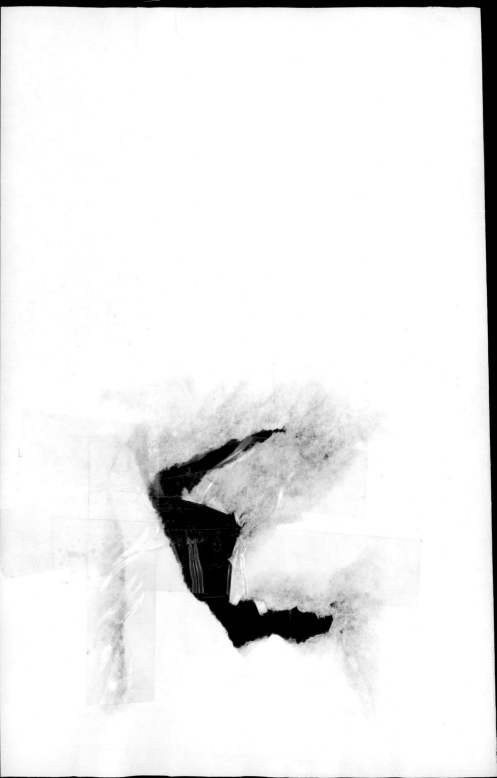

Culture
and Civility
in San Francisco

*trans***action books**

TA-1   Campus Power Struggle/*Howard S. Becker*

TA-2   Cuban Communism/*Irving Louis Horowitz*

TA-3   The Changing South/*Raymond W. Mack*

TA-4   Where Medicine Fails/*Anselm L. Strauss*

TA-5   The Sexual Scene/*John H. Gagnon and William Simon*

TA-6   Black Experience: Soul/*Lee Rainwater*

TA-7   Black Experience: The Transformation of Activism/*August Meier*

TA-8   Law and Order: Modern Criminals/*James F. Short, Jr.*

TA-9   Law and Order: The Scales of Justice/*Abraham S. Blumberg*

TA-10 Social Science and National Policy/*Fred R. Harris*

TA-11 Peace and the War Industry/*Kenneth E. Boulding*

TA-12 America and the Asian Revolutions/*Robert Jay Lifton*

TA-13 Law and Order: Police Encounters/*Michael Lipsky*

TA-14 American Bureaucracy/*Warren G. Bennis*

TA-15 The Values of Social Science/*Norman K. Denzin*

TA-16 Ghetto Revolts/*Peter H. Rossi*

TA-17 The Future Society/*Donald N. Michael*

TA-18 Awakening Minorities: American Indians, Mexican Americans, Puerto Ricans/*John R. Howard*

TA-19 The American Military/*Martin Oppenheimer*

TA-20 Total Institutions/*Samuel E. Wallace*

TA-21 The Anti-American Generation/*Edgar Z. Friedenberg*

TA-22 Religion in Radical Transition/*Jeffrey K. Hadden*

TA-23 Culture and Civility in San Francisco/*Howard S. Becker*

TA-24 Poor Americans: How the White Poor Live/*Marc Pilisuk and Phyllis Pilisuk*

Culture
and Civility
in San Francisco

Edited by

HOWARD S. BECKER

*trans*action Books
339697
Distributed by
Aldine Publishing Company

The essays in this book originally appeared
in the April 1970 issue of *trans* **action** Magazine

TA Book 23
Library of Congress Catalog Number 73-133310

Contents

Preface   ix

Introduction   1
Howard S. Becker

THE CULTURE OF CIVILITY   4
Howard S. Becker/Irving Louis Horowitz

RED GUARD ON GRANT AVENUE   20
Stanford M. Lyman

THE GAME OF BLACK AND WHITE AT HUNTERS POINT   53
Arthur E. Hippler

SAN FRANCISCO: A PHOTOGRAPHIC PORTFOLIO   76
Michael Alexander

THE HEALTH OF HAIGHT-ASHBURY   77
David E. Smith/John Luce/Ernest A. Dernburg

THE POLITICS OF HYPERPLURALISM   101
Frederick M. Wirt

STORE FRONT LAWYERS IN SAN FRANCISCO   125
Jerome E. Carlin

THE SAN FRANCISCO MYSTIQUE   151
Fred Davis

Notes on Contributors   162

Preface

However diverse their attitudes and interpretations may sometimes be, social scientists are now entering a period of shared realization that the United States—both at home and abroad—has entered a crucial period of transition. Indeed, the much burdened word "crisis" has now become a commonplace among black militants, Wall Street lawyers, housewives, and even professional politicians.

For the past eight years, *trans*action magazine has dedicated itself to the task of reporting the strains and conflicts within the American system. But the magazine has done more than this. It has pioneered in social programs for changing the society, offered the kind of analysis that has permanently restructured the terms of the "dialogue" between peoples and publics, and offered the sort of prognosis that makes for real alterations in social and political policies directly affecting our lives.

The work done in the pages of *trans*action has crossed professional boundaries. This represents much more than simple cross-disciplinary "team efforts." It embodies rather a recognition that the social world cannot be easily carved into neat academic areas. That, indeed, the study of the experience of blacks in American ghettos, or the manifold uses and abuses of agencies of law enforcement, or the sorts of overseas policies that lead to the celebration of some dictatorships and the condemnation of others, can best be examined from many viewpoints and from the vantage points of many disciplines.

This series of books clearly demonstrates the superiority of starting with real world problems and searching out practical solutions, over the zealous guardianship of professional boundaries. Indeed, it is precisely this approach that has elicited enthusiastic support from leading American social scientists for this new and dynamic series.

The demands upon scholarship and scientific judgment are particularly stringent, for no one has been untouched by the current situation. Each essay republished in these volumes bears the imprint of the author's attempt to communicate his own experience of the crisis. Yet, despite the sense of urgency these papers exhibit, the editors feel that many have withstood the test of time, and match in durable interest the best of available social science literature. This collection of *trans*action articles, then, attempts to address itself to immediate issues without violating the basic insights derived from the classical literature in the various fields of social science.

The subject matter of these books concerns social changes that have aroused the longstanding needs and present-day anxieties of us all. These changes are in organizational life styles, concepts of human ability and intelligence, changing patterns of norms and morals, the relationship of social conditions to physical and biological environments, and in the status of social science with national policy making.

The dissident minorities, massive shifts in norms of social conduct, population explosions and urban expansions, and vast realignments between nations of the world of recent years do not promise to disappear in the seventies. But the social scientists involved as editors and authors of this *trans*action series have gone beyond observation of these critical areas, and have entered into the vital and difficult tasks of explanation and interpretation. They have defined issues in a way making solutions possible. They have provided answers as well as asked the right questions. Thus, this series should be conceived as the first collection dedicated not to highlighting social problems alone, but to establishing guidelines for social solutions based on the social sciences.

THE EDITORS
*trans*action

Introduction

HOWARD S. BECKER

Another book about San Francisco?
Yes.
Is it all about the cable cars and the good cheap restaurants and how beautiful the Bay is?
No.
What then?
Well, it's about whores and Chinatown and—
I knew it, another tourist guide!
No, not a tourist guide. It's a book about city life. Everybody says that San Francisco is different, and we have tried in this book to explain a little of what the difference is, in a way that takes advantage of modern social science thinking. We think that, quite apart from the cable cars and the bridges and all the rest of the standard romantic picture of The City, San Francisco is different, in ways that are relevant to an understanding of the troubles of modern cities. San Francisco differs just enough from other American cities to allow us to glimpse some possibilities that

1

have not been explored as fully elsewhere.

Like what?

Like it's probably more tolerant of odd behavior, of dope smoking and freaky sex, of alternate life styles, than most big cities. Horowitz and Becker, in "The Culture of Civilty," make much of this, arguing that some lessons about how groups with different interests can find a way of living together lie in an analysis of that tolerance's workings. Davis, in "The San Francisco Mystique," gets into the ideology that goes with that tolerance, the emphasis on variety that makes deviance not merely tolerable but a good thing, to be encouraged and sought after.

Of course, that kind of thing may make The City more colorful for some, more fun for others, more peaceful for many, but it doesn't solve all the problems. San Francisco has plenty of poor people, and all the color in the world won't help them. One of the things that makes San Francisco particularly interesting is that some of the most imaginative experiments in trying to provide help to people who need it are taking place there. Carlin, in "Store Front Lawyers in San Francisco," describes the experience of the Neighborhood Legal Assistance Foundation. The Foundation has provided the legal muscle needed to make poor people active participants in the urban struggle by giving them a better break vis-á-vis city government in the courts.

Another important experiment is the Haight-Ashbury Free Medical Clinic, which undertook to provide the medical care that largely hippie community needed, on terms its inhabitants were willing to accept. People who are concerned about the "delivery of health services" might learn a lot by examining the Clinic's successes and troubles, reported in Luce, Smith and Dernberg's "The Health of Haight-Ashbury."

You're right, this doesn't sound like a tourist book.

It isn't. It's about city life, and city life is politics. The other articles get into that even more explicitly. Frederick Wirt talks about "The Politics of Hyperpluralsim," the difficulty city government has in getting anything done when power is fragmented in the way the theory of pluralism recommends. And while every tourist book tells about Chinatown, they don't tell you about the fights for political power inside that community, vividly analyzed by Lyman in "Red Guard on Grant Avenue." None of them ever mentions the black community—

That's no tourist attraction!

—but Hippler explains its inner workings in "The Game of Black and White at Hunter's Point."

Do you at least have pictures?

Not just pictures. We have a photographic essay by Michael Alexander, whose strong images make their own statement about life in The City.

There is a lot more to say about San Francisco than gets said here. We could have applied—and perhaps another time will—the same approach to crime and the police, to education, to the arts, to urban conservation, to the radio, television and press, both respectable and underground. They all reflect the difference of San Francisco and contribute to it. For the present, what we have done will suffice to show why an analysis of San Francisco's past and present can help us not only to understand everyone's favorite city a little better, but also to understand all cities.

San Francisco
August, 1970

The Culture of Civility

HOWARD S. BECKER/IRVING LOUIS HOROWITZ

Deviants of many kinds live well in San Francisco—natives and tourists alike make that observation. The city's apparently casual and easygoing response to "sex, dope and cheap thrills" (to crib the suppressed full title of Janis Joplin's famous album—itself a San Francisco product) astounds visitors from other parts of the country who can scarcely credit either what they see happening or the way natives stroll by those same events unconcerned.

□ Walking in the Tenderloin on a summer evening, a block from the Hilton, you hear a black whore cursing at a policeman: "I wasn't either blocking the sidewalk! Why don't you motherfucking fuzz mind your own goddamn business!" The visiting New Yorker expects to see her arrested, if not shot, but the cop smiles good-naturedly and moves on, having got her back into the doorway where she is supposed to be.

□ You enter one of the famous rock ballrooms and, as you stand getting used to the noise and lights, someone puts a lit joint of marijuana in your hand. The tourist looks for someplace to hide, not wishing to be caught in the mass arrest he expects to follow. No need to worry. The police will not come in, knowing if they do they will have to arrest people and create disorder.

☐ Candidates for the city's Board of Supervisors make their pitch for the homosexual vote, estimated by some at 90,000. They will not be run out of town; the candidates' remarks are dutifully reported in the daily paper, as are the evaluations of them by representatives of SIR, the Society for Individual Rights.

☐ The media report (tongue in cheek) the annual Halloween Drag Ball, for which hundreds of homosexuals turn out at one of the city's major hotels in full regalia, unharassed by police.

☐ One sees long-haired, bearded hippies all over the city, not just in a few preserves set aside for them. Straight citizens do not remark their presence, either by gawking, hostility or flight.

☐ Nudie movies, frank enough to satisfy anyone's curiosity, are exhibited in what must be the largest number of specialty movie houses per capita in the country. Periodic police attempts to close them down (one of the few occasions when repression has been attempted) fail.

The items can be multiplied indefinitely, and their multiplicity demands explanation. Most cities in the United States refuse to let deviants indulge themselves publicly, let alone tolerate candidates who seek their bloc votes. Quite the contrary. Other cities, New York and Chicago being good examples, would see events like these as signs of serious trouble, omens of a real breakdown in law enforcement and deviance control, the forerunner of saturnalia and barbarian take-over. Because its politicians and police allow and can live with activities that would freak their opposite numbers elsewhere, San Francisco is a natural experiment in the consequences of tolerating deviance. We can see from its example what happens when we ignore the warnings of the custodians of conventional morality. We can learn too about the conditions under which problems that perhaps lie deeper than matters of morals or life style can be solved to the satisfaction of all the parties to them.

We can summarize this low-key approach to deviance in the phrase "a culture of civility." What are its components, and how does it maintain itself?

San Francisco prides itself on its sophistication, on being the most European of American cities, on its picturesque cosmopolitanism. The picturesque quality, indeed the quaintness, rests in part on physical beauty. As the filling of the Bay and the destruction of the skyline by high-rise buildings proceeds to destroy that beauty, the city has come to depend even more on the presence of undigested ethnic minorities. It is as though San Francisco did not wish its Italians, Chinese or Russians to assimilate and become standard Americans, preferring instead to maintain a panoply of ethnic differences: religious, cultural and culinary (especially culinary). A sophisticated, livable city, on this view, contains people, colonies and societies of all kinds. Their differences create a mosaic of life styles, the very difference of whose sight and smell give pleasure.

Like ethnic minorities, deviant minorities create enclaves whose differences add to the pleasure of city life. Natives enjoy the presence of hippies and take tourists to see their areas, just as they take them to see the gay area of Polk Street. Deviance, like difference, is a civic resource, enjoyed by tourist and resident alike.

To enjoy deviance instead of fearing it requires a surrender of some common sense notions about the world. Most people assume, when they see someone engaging in proscribed activity, that there is worse to come. "Anyone who would do that [take dope, dress in women's clothes, sell his body or whatever] would do anything" is the major premise of the syllogism. "If you break one law or convention, who knows where you'll stop." Common sense ignores the contrary cases around us everywhere: professional criminals often flourish a legionnaire's patriotism; housewives in every other respect conventional sometimes shoplift; homosexuals may be good family providers; some people who habitually use the rings from poptop cans to work the parking meter would not dream of taking dope, and vice versa. Deviance, like conforming behavior, is highly selective. San Francisco's culture of civility, accepting that premise, assumes that if I know that you steal or take dope or peddle your ass, that is all I *know*. There may be more to know; then again, there may be nothing. The deviant may be perfectly decent in every other respect. We are often enjoined, in a generalization of therapeutic doctrine, to treat other people as individuals; the prescription comes nearer to being filled in San Francisco than in most places in the United States.

Because of that tolerance, deviants find it possible to live somewhat more openly in San Francisco than elsewhere. People do not try so hard to catch them at their deviant activities and are less likely to punish them when caught. Because they live more openly, what they do is more visible to straight members of the community. An established canon of social psychology tells us that we find it harder to maintain negative sterotypes when our personal experience belies them. We see more clearly and believe more deeply that hippies or homosexuals are not dangerous when we confront them on the street day after day or live alongside them and realize that beard plus long hair does not equal a drug-crazed maniac, that limp wrist plus lisp does not equal child-molester.

When such notions become embodied in a culture of

civility, the citizenry begins to sense that "everyone" feels that way. We cannot say at what critical point a population senses that sophistication about deviance is the norm, rather than a liberal fad. But San Francisco clearly has that critical mass. To come on as an anti-deviant, in a way that would probably win friends and influence voters in more parochial areas, risks laughter and ridicule in San Francisco. Conservatives who believe in law and order are thus inclined to keep their beliefs to themselves. The more people keep moralistic notions to themselves, the more everyone believes that tolerance is widespread. The culture maintains itself by convincing the populace that it is indeed the culture.

It gets help from public pronouncements of civic officials, who enunciate what will be taken as the collective sentiment of the city. San Francisco officials occasionally angle for the conservative vote that disapproves licentiousness. But they more frequently take the side of liberty, if not license. When the police, several years ago, felt compelled to close the first of the "topless joints," the judge threw the case out. He reasoned that Supreme Court decisions required him to take into account contemporary community standards. In his judgment San Francisco was not a prudish community; case dismissed. The city's major paper, the *Chronicle,* approved. Few protested.

Similarly, when California's leading Yahoo, Superintendent of Public Instruction Max Rafferty, threatened to revoke the teaching credentials of any San Francisco teacher who used the obscene materials listed in the standard high school curriculum (Eldridge Cleaver's *Soul on Ice* and LeRoi Jones' *Dutchman*), the City did not remove the offending books from its curriculum. Instead, it successfully sued to have Rafferty enjoined from interfering in its operation.

In short, San Franciscans know that they are supposed to

be sophisticated and let that knowledge guide their public actions, whatever their private feelings. According to another well-known law of social psychology, their private feelings often come to resemble their public actions, and they learn to delight in what frightens citizens of less civil cities.

We do not suggest that all kinds of deviation are tolerated endlessly. The police try, in San Francisco as elsewhere, to stamp out some vices and keep a ceiling on others. Some deviants frighten San Franciscans too, precisely because their activities seem to portend worse to come (most recently, users and purveyors of methedrine—"speed merchants" and "speed freaks"—whose drug use is popularly thought to result in violence and crime). But the line is drawn much farther over on the side of "toleration" in San Francisco than elsewhere. A vastly wider range of activities is publicly acceptable. Despite the wide range of visible freakiness, the citizenry takes it all in stride, without the fear and madness that permeates the conventional sectors of cities like Detroit, Chicago, New York, Washington, D.C. and similar centers of undaunted virtue.

How does a culture of civility arise? Here we can only speculate, and then fragmentarily, since so few cities in the United States have one that we cannot make the comparisons that might uncover the crucial conditions. San Francisco's history suggests a number of possibilities.

It has, for one thing, a Latin heritage. Always a major seaport, it has long tolerated the vice that caters to sailors typical of such ports. It grew at the time of the gold rush in an explosive way that burst through conventional social controls. It ceded to its ethnic minorities, particularly the Chinese, the right to engage in prostitution, gambling and other activities. Wickedness and high living form part of the prized past every "tourist" city constructs for itself; some minor downtown streets in San Francisco, for instance, are named for famous madames of the gold rush era.

Perhaps more important, a major potential source of repressive action—the working class—is in San Francisco more libertarian and politically sophisticated than one might expect. Harry Bridges' longshoremen act as bellwethers. San Francisco is one of the few major American cities ever to experience a general strike and the event still reverberates. Working people who might support repression of others know by personal experience that the policeman may not be their friend. Trade unionism has a left-wing, honest base which gives the city a working-class democracy and even eccentricity, rather than the customary pattern of authoritarianism.

Finally, San Francisco is a town of single people. Whatever actual proportion of the adult population is married, the city's culture is oriented toward and organized for single people. As a consequence, citizens worry less about what public deviance will do to their children, for they don't have any and don't intend to, or they move from the city when they do. (Since there are, of course, plenty of families in the city, it may be more accurate to say that there are fewer white middle-class families, that being the stratum that would, if family-based, provide the greatest number of complaints about deviance. Black, chicano and oriental populations ordinarily have enough to worry about without becoming guardians of public morality.)

San Francisco is known across the country as a haven for deviants. Good homosexuals hope to go to San Francisco to stay when they die, if not before. Indeed, one of the problems of deviant communities in San Francisco is coping with the periodic influx of a new generation of bohemians who have heard that it is the place to be: the beatnik migration of the late fifties and the hippie hordes of 1967. But those problems should not obscure what is more important: that there are stable communities of some size there to be disrupted. It is the stable homosexual community that promises politicians 90,000 votes and the stable bohemian communities of several vintages that provide both personnel and customers for some important local industries (developing, recording and distributing rock music is now a business of sizeable proportions).

Stable communities are stable because their members have found enough of what they want to stay where they are for a while. If where they were proved totally unsatisfying, they presumably would move elsewhere, unless restrained. But no one forces deviants to live in San Francisco. They stay there because it offers them, via the culture of civility, a place to live where they are not shunned as fearsome or disgusting, where agents of control (police and others) do not regard them as unfortunate excrescences to be excised at the first opportunity. Because they have a place to stay that does not harass them, they sink roots like more conventional citizens: find jobs, buy houses, make friends, vote and take part in political activities and all the other things that solid citizens do.

Sinking roots stabilizes deviants' lives, as it does the lives of conventional citizens. They find less need to act in the erratic ways deviants often behave elsewhere, less need to fulfill the prophecy that because they are deviant in one respect they will be deviant in other, more dangerous ways. San Francisco employers know that homosexuals make good employees. Why not? They are not likely to be blackmailed by enterprising hustlers. The police seldom haul them off to jail for little reason or beat them because they feel like pushing some "queers" around. Homosexuals fear none of this in San Francisco, or fear it much less than in most places, and so are less given to the overcompensatory "camping" that gets their fellows into trouble elsewhere.

Police and others do not harass deviants because they

have found, though they may deny it for public relations purposes, that looking the other way is sometimes a good policy. It is easier, when a Be-In is going on, to turn your back on the sight of open marijuana smoking than it is to charge into the crowd and try to arrest people who will destroy the evidence before you get there, give you a hard time, make a fool of you and earn you a bad press—and leave you with no conviction to show for it. At the same time, when you turn your back, nothing worse is likely to happen: no muggings, no thefts, no rapes, no riots. Police, more calculating than they seem, often choose just this kind of accommodation with stable deviant communities.

The accommodation works in circular fashion. When deviants can live decent lives, they find it possible to behave decently. Furthermore, they acquire the kind of stake they are often denied elsewhere in the present and future structure of the community. That stake constrains them to behave in ways that will not outrage nondeviants, for they do not want to lose what they have. They moderate their activities to what they think the community will stand for.

The community in turn, and especially the police, will put up with more than they might otherwise, because they understand that nothing else is forthcoming, and because they find that what they are confronted with is not so bad after all. If homosexuals have a Halloween Drag Ball, the community discovers it can treat it as a good-natured joke; those who are offended discover that they needn't go near the Hilton while it is happening.

No doubt neither party to such a bargain gets quite what he would like. Straight members of the community presumably would prefer not to have whores walking the downtown streets, would prefer not to have gay bars operating openly. Deviants of all kinds presumably would prefer not to have to make any concessions to straight sensibilities. Each gives up something and gets something, and to that degree the arrangement becomes stable, the stability itself something both prize.

What we have just described verges on the idyllic, Peace and Harmony in Camelot forever. Such a dream of perfection does not exist in San Francisco, though more deviants there have more of the advantages of such a bargain, perhaps, than in any other city in the United States. Nor is it clear that the system we described, even in its perfect form, would be such an idyll.

In San Francisco, as everywhere, the forces of decency and respectability draw the line somewhere and can be every bit as forceful and ruthless the other side of that line as the forces of decency and respectability anywhere else. When Haight-Ashbury got "out of hand" with the overcrowded transiency of 1967, the city moved in the police Tactical Squad, the City Health Department and all the other bureaucratic weapons usually used to rouse deviants. They did it again with the growth of violence in that area associated with the use and sale of methedrine. In general, the city has responded with great toughness to those deviants it believes will not be satisfied with something "reasonable." In particular, political dissent has sometimes been met with force, though San Francisco police have never indulged themselves in the way that has made Chicago police internationally detested.

The system has beauty only for those deviants who do not mind giving up some portion of their liberty, and then only if what they are willing to give up is the same as what the community wants given up. This no doubt is the reason an accommodative system works well with those whose deviant desires are narrowly circumscribed, and may have less utility with those whose wants can be accommodated only at the expense of others who will not easily give up their privileges. In fact, many current urban difficulties clearly result from the breakdown of accommodation.

These considerations indicate the more general importance of San Francisco's experiment in tolerating and accommodating to the minor forms of deviance encompassed in sex, dope and cheap thrills. How can a complex and differentiated society deal with variety and dissent and simultaneously with its own urges for centralized control? An accommodative relationship to difference, in which it is allowed to persist while paying some minimal dues to the whole, is what San Francisco recommends to us, suggesting that the amount of the dues and the breadth of the license be set where both parties will, for the time being, stand still for it. The resulting working arrangement will be at least temporarily stable and provide for all concerned a tranquility that permits one to go about his business unharmed that many will find attractive.

But is this no more than a clever trick, a way of buying off deviant populations with minor freedoms while still keeping them enslaved? Beneath the rhetoric, the analysis is the same. The more radical statement adds only that the people who accept such a bargain ought not to, presumably because they have, if they only knew it, deeper and more important interests and desires which remain unsatisfied in the accommodative arrangement. So, of course, do those who hold them in check. Perhaps that is the ultimate lesson of San Francisco: the price of civilization, civility and living together peacefully is not getting everything you want.

It is tempting to think that an accommodation based on civility and mutual interest provides a model for settling the conflicts now wracking our urban areas. Our analysis suggests that this is a possibility, but no more than that. Peace can occur through accommodation, the example of the potheads and pimps tells us, only under certain not so easily attained conditions. Those conditions may not be present in the ethnic and political problems our major cities, San Francisco among them, are now experiencing.

Accommodation requires, as a first condition, that the parties involved prize peace and stability enough to give up some of what they want so that others may have their desires satisfied as well. But people take that point of view only when the accommodation leaves them enough of a share to want no more. Some urban groups no longer believe that they are getting that necessary minimum, either because they have learned to interpret their situation in a new light or because they have lost some advantages they once had.

Members of black communities may be no worse off than ever, but they are considerably worse off than whites and know it. For a variety of historical reasons, and as a matter of simple justice, some of them no longer regard the little they have as sufficient reason to keep the peace. All the discussion about how many blacks feel this way (is it 10 percent or 50 percent?) and how strongly they feel it (are they willing to fight?) is beside the main point: enough feel strongly enough to make a lot of trouble for the white community, thus changing the balance of costs to whites and insisting on a new division of rights as the price of stability.

Some members of white communities probably are objectively worse off and may resent it sufficiently to give up peace and stability in an effort to raise the costs to others and thus minimize their losses. Many whites in civil service positions, in the skilled trades and in similar protected occupational positions have lost or are in danger of losing competitive job advantages as governments act to do something about the injustice that afflicts black communities. Without a general expansion of the economy, which is *not* what blacks demand, injustices inflicted on blacks can be remedied only by taking something away from more favorably situated whites. It may be possible to improve the education of poor black children, for instance, only by taking away some of the privileges of white teachers. It may be possible to give black youths a chance at apprenticeships in skilled trades only by removing the privileged access to those positions of the sons of present white union members. When whites lose those privileges, they may feel strongly enough to fracture the consensus of civility.

The deviant communities of San Francisco show us cases in which the parties involved agree in a way that leaves each enough. But that may only be possible when the interests to be accommodated involve morals and life styles. When those interests include substantial economic prizes, major forms of privilege and real political power, it may be that nothing less than a real-life assessment of relative intensities of desire and ability to inflict costs on others will suffice. That assessment takes place in the marketplace of conflict.

This suggests a second, more procedural condition for the achievement of urban peace through accommodation and civility. Mechanisms and procedures must exist by which the conflicting desires and resources for bargaining can be brought together to produce a temporarily stable working arrangement. The accommodations of enforcement officials and deviants typically occur in a host of minor bargaining situations. Hassles are settled by the people immediately involved, and settled "on their own merits"— in a way, that is, that respects the strength of everyone's feelings and the amount of trouble each is prepared to make to have his way. The culture of civility works well because the myriad of separate local bargains respect and reflect what most of the involved parties want or are willing to settle for.

We do not allow ourselves this extreme degree of decentralized decision-making with respect to many important problems (though many critics have suggested we should).

Instead, we allow federal, state or city bureaucracies to make general policies that inhibit local accommodation. While government might well intervene when circumstances make bargaining positions unequal, we know now that it is not ordinarily well equipped to reach accommodative agreements that will work at the grass roots. Unable to know what the people who inhabit local areas will want and settle for, officials turn to technocrats for solutions.

Thus, when we confront the problem of slums and urban renewal, we send for the planner and the bulldozer. But the lives of urban residents are not determined by the number or newness of buildings. The character of their relationships with one another and with the outside world does that. Planners and technocrats typically ignore those relationships, and their influence in shaping what people want, in constructing solutions. They define "slums" impersonally, using such impersonal criteria as density or deterioration, and fail to see how awakened group consciousness can turn a "slum" into a "ghetto," and a rise in moral repute turn a "ghetto" into a "neighborhood."

Too often, the search for "model cities" implies not so much a model as an ideology—a rationalistic vision of human interaction that implies a people whose consistency of behavior can nowhere be found. We already have "model cities": Brasilia at the bureaucratic end and Levittown at the residential end. And in both instances the force of human impulses had to break through the web of formal models to make these places inhabitable. In Brasilia the rise of shantytown dwellings outside the federal buildings made the place "a city," whereas the Levittowners had to break the middle-class mode and pass through a generation of conformity before they could produce a decent living arrangement. To design a city in conformity to "community standards"—which turn out to be little more than the prejudices of building inspectors, housing designers and absentee landlords—only reinforces patterns of frustration, violence and antagonism that now characterize so many of America's large cities. To think that the dismal failure of large housing projects will be resolved by their dismal replacement by small housing projects is nonsense. Minibuildings are no more a solution than maxibuildings are the problem.

In any event, centralized planning operating in this way does not produce a mechanism through which the mutual desires, claims and threats of interested groups can sort themselves out and allow a *modus vivendi,* if one exists, to uncover itself. The centralized body makes bargains for everyone under its influence, without knowing their circumstances or wants, and so makes it impossible for the people involved to reach a stable accommodation. But centralized planning still remains a major solution proffered for urban problems of every kind.

Accommodations reached through the mechanism of old-fashioned city political machines work little better, for contemporary machines typically fail to encompass all the people whose interests are at stake. Richard Daley demonstrated that when the Chicago ghetto, supposedly solidly under his control, exploded and revealed some people his famed consensus had not included. Lyndon Johnson made the same discovery with respect to opponents of the Vietnam War. Insofar as centralized decision-making does not work, and interested parties are not allowed to make bargains at the local level, accommodative stability cannot occur.

So the example of San Francisco's handling of moral deviance may not provide the blueprint one would like for settling urban problems generally. Its requirements include a day-to-day working agreement among parties on the value of compromise and a procedure by which their immediate interests can be openly communicated and effectively adjusted. Those requirements are difficult to meet. Yet it may be that they are capable of being met in more places than we think, that even some of the knottier racial and political problems contain possibilities of accommodation, no more visible to us than the casual tolerance of deviance in San Francisco was thinkable to some of our prudish forebearers.

Red Guard on Grant Avenue

STANFORD M. LYMAN

Visitors to San Francisco's historic Portsmouth Square on May 7, 1969 were startled to see the flag of the People's Republic of China flying over the plaza. The occasion had begun as a rally to commemorate the 50th anniversary of the May 4 movement in Peking, when Chinese students demonstrated to protest the ignominious treaties forced on a moribund Chinese Empire by Occidental imperialists. Now a half century later in San Francisco, a group of disaffected Chinatown youth took over the rally from its sponsors to protest against the community's poverty and neglect and to criticize its anachronistic and conservative power elite.

Calling themselves the Red Guards, the youths asserted their right to armed self-defense against the city police and called for the release of all Asians in city, state and federal prisons on the ground that they had had unfair trials. On a more immediate and practical level, the Red Guards announced plans for a remarkably unradical petition cam-

paign to prevent the Chinese Playground from being con-
verted into a garage and for a breakfast program to aid
needy children in the Chinatown ghetto. If the platform
of the Red Guards sounded vaguely familiar, a spokesman
for the group made it plain: "The Black Panthers are the
most revolutionary group in the country and we are pat-
terned after them."

To most San Franciscans the rise of youthful rebellion
in the Chinese quarter of the city must come as a surprise.
For the past three decades Chinese-Americans have been
stereotyped in the mass media as quiet, docile and filial,
a people who are as unlikely to espouse radicalism as they
are to permit delinquency among their juveniles. In the
last few years, however, evidence has mounted to suggest
a discrepancy between this somewhat saccharine imagery
and reality. Not only is there an unmistakable increase
in delinquent activity among Chinese young people, there
is a growing restlessness among them as well. Chinatown's
younger generation feels a gnawing frustration over hide-
bound local institutions, the powerlessness of youth and
their own bleak prospects for the future. The politics as
well as the "crimes" of Chinatown are coming to resemble
those of the larger society, with alienation, race consciousness and restive rebelliousness animating a new generation's social and organizational energies.

A basic cause for the emergence of youthful rebellion
among the Chinese is the increase in the youthful population itself. There are simply more Chinese youth in the
ghetto now than there ever have been before, a fact that
can be attributed to an increasing birth rate among the
indigenous population and a sudden rise in immigration
from Hong Kong and other Asian centers of Chinese
settlement.

By 1890, eight years after a wave of sinophobia had
prompted Congress to block any further immigration of

Chinese to this country, there were approximately 102,620 residents here. The vast majority were laborers or small merchants lured here by the promise of the "Gold Mountain" in California and work on the railroads. But a more significant fact is that the vast majority were also men. Before the turn of the century there were about 27 men for every woman among the Chinese in America. What this meant for white perceptions of these newcomers is probably familiar enough. Forced into ghettos, their women and children left behind to care for and honor their parents, these men joined together in clan associations and secret societies to provide them with some sense of familiarity and solidarity; and they turned as well to the typical pleasures of lonely men—prostitutes, stupefaction (through opium) and gambling. Just as typically, in a society known for its hostile racial stereotypes, the Chinese came to be identified with these "vices" in the minds of many white Americans and to be regarded as bestial, immoral and dangerous. But the alarming imbalance in the sex ratio also meant that the Chinese communities in America were almost incapable of producing a second generation of American-born Chinese. It wasn't until 1950 that the American-born made up more than half the total Chinese population, and even this growth only came about through the small trickle of illegal entries made by Chinese women prior to 1943 and the much larger number who entered since that date, thanks to gradual but important relaxations of the immigration laws.

The most radical of these relaxations came with the Immigration Act of 1965 which repealed the entire system of quotas based on national origins and substituted an entry procedure based on skills and the reuniting of families. Under this law, according to District Immigration Director C. W. Fullilove, there will be approximately 1,200 Chinese entering San Francisco every year with the intention of staying here. Although not all of them will do so, this new influx of Chinese makes up a significant proportion of San Francisco's burgeoning Chinese population, and many of them fall between what Fullilove calls "the problem ages" for Chinese youth, 16 to 19.

Of course, sheer numbers alone do not account for the rise of rebelliousness among young Chinese in San Francisco. A more significant factor is that conditions of life in Chinatown are by no means pleasant, productive or promising. We must distinguish, however, from among the Chinese those who have escaped the ghetto, those who are American born but who still inhabit Chinatown and those foreign-born youth who reluctantly find themselves imprisoned within a ghetto even less of their own making then it is of the others'. Among those who have escaped there are, first, the scholars, scientists, intellectuals and professionals—many of whom hail from regions other than southeastern China, the original home of the bulk of America's Chinese immigrants—who have found work and residence within the larger society. Enclosed in university, corporation, professional or government communities, these Chinese do not for the most part feel themselves to be a part of Chinatown; they go there only occasionally for a banquet or for a brief sense of their ethnic origins. A second group much larger than the first, although actually quite small in relation to the total number of Chinese, consists of those American-born Chinese who have successfully completed high school and college and gone on to enter the professions—most frequently pharmacy and engineering—the American middle class and, when they can evade or circumvent the still prevalent discrimination in housing, the finer neighborhoods or the suburbs. This "gold bourgeoisie"—to paraphrase E. Franklin Frazier—is also estranged from Chinatown. Proud of his own achievements, wary of any attempt to thrust him back into a confining ghetto existence and alternately angered, embarrassed or shamed by the presence of alienated, hostile and rebellious youth in Chinatown, the middle-class American Chinese holds tenaciously to his newly achieved material and social success.

Nevertheless, middle-class native-born Chinese are discovering that the American dream is not an unmixed blessing. The "Gold Mountain" of American bourgeios promise seems somehow less glittering now that its actual pinnacle has been reached. Chinese, like other descendants of immigrants in America, are discovering that the gold is alloyed more heavily than they had supposed with brass; but, like their second and third generation peers among the Jews and Japanese, they are not quite sure what to do about it. The price of success has been very great—not the least payments being the abandonment of language, culture and much of their ethnic identity. Among some there is a new search for cultural roots in Chinese history, a strong desire to recover the ancient arts and a renewed interest in speaking Chinese—at least at home. Others emphasize, perhaps with too much protestation, their happiness within the American middle class and carry on a conspicuous consumption of leisure to prove it. Finally, a few recognize their Chinatown roots and return there with a desire to aid somehow in the advancement of the Chinese ghetto-dwellers. Sometimes their offers of help are rejected with curses by the objects of their solicitude, but in any event the growing number of restive Chinatowners constitutes another challenge to the comfort of bourgeois Chinese.

In its most primordial sense the visible contrast between the style of life of the impoverished ghetto-dweller and that of the middle-class professional promotes guilt and shame. Somehow it seems wrong that one's ethnic compatriots should suffer while one enjoys the benefits of success. Yet middle-class Chinese are quite ready to attribute their success to their own diligence, proverbial habits of thrift and hard work and to their conscious avoidance of delinquent or other kinds of unruly behavior. Naturally, then, some middle-class Chinese are equally quick to charge the angry Chinatown youth with indolence, impropriety and impiety. But even as they preach the old virtues as a sure cure for the young people's personal and social ailments, some perceive that there is more to these problems than can be solved by the careful nurturing of Confucian or Protestant ethics. They see more clearly than the Americanized and less alienated Chinese of the fifties that poverty, cultural deprivation and discrimination are truly obdurate barriers to the advancement of the ghetto-dwellers of today. Moreover, there is an even more profound problem. Like other alienated youthful minorities, the youth of Chinatown appear to reject just that dream which inspired and activated the now bourgeois Chinese. For the middle-class Chinese, then, the peak of the "Gold Mountain" seems to have been reached just when those still down below started to shout up that the arduous climb isn't worth the effort.

Among Chinatown's rebellious groups there are two distinguishable types of youth—those who are American-born but have dropped out of school and form part of the under- or unemployed proletariat of the Chinese community; and those recently arrived immigrant youth who, speaking little or no English and having little to offer in the way of salable skills, find themselves unable to enter the city's occupational and social mainstream. Both native and foreign-born Chinese are included among the ranks of the quasi-criminal and quasi-political gangs that are accused of contributing to the mounting incidence of delinquency in the Chinese quarter. Culture, language and background have divided the native from the foreign-born Chinese in the past, and it is only recently that there is any sign of a common recognition between the two groups.

It is traditional to focus on Chinatown gangs as an unfortunate form of juvenile delinquency among a people otherwise noted for their social quiescence and honesty. A more fruitful approach however would adopt the perspective taken by E. J. Hobsbawm in his discussion of social bandits and primitive rebels. According to Hobsbawm, who has studied these phenomena in Europe, social banditry is a form of pre-ideological rebellion which arises among essentially agrarian, unskilled and unlettered peoples who are at great cultural distance from the official and oppressive power structure. It is led by those who enjoy a certain amount of local notoriety or awe. Often enough social banditry remains at a stage of petty criminality which is of concern, if at all, only to the local police. At a more refined stage, however, predatory gangs are formed which confine their criminal activities to attacks on strangers and officials and share any loot with local community members who, though not a party to the attacks, identify with and protect the robbers.

It is important to note that bandit gangs may adopt a populist or a conservative style. The former is symbolized by Robin Hood, who robbed the rich to feed the poor and attacked civic or state officialdom as intruders in the community's traditional way of life. In the conservative style, bandit gangs are co-opted as toughs and thugs to defend local satrapies and powerful petty interests. Social banditry may exist side by side with ideologically rebellious or revolutionary elements but is usually untouched by them except for particular reasons of strategy or tactics. Essentially, it is separated from ideological politics by its deep involvement with local ethnic rather than cosmopolitan class interests. However, it is not impossible for class and ethnic interests to merge and for the liberation of local groups to become enmeshed within the revolutionary aims of a radically politicized sector of a modern party state.

From the perspective of "primitive rebellion," Chinatown's gangs take on a greater significance for the understanding of loosely structured pluralistic societies like the United States. Gangs in Chinatown are by no means a new phenomenon, but their activities in the past describe mainly the early stages of social banditry. For the most part Chinatown's traditional social banditry has been of a particularly conservative type, identified with the recruitment of young toughs, thugs and bullies into the small criminal arm of Chinatown's secret societies. They formed the "flying squads" of mercenaries who "protected" brothels, guarded gambling establishments and enforced secret society monopolies over other vice institutions of Chinatown. From their numbers came assassins and strong-arm men who fought in the so-called tong wars that characterized Chinatown's internecine struggles of a half century ago and which still occasionally threaten to erupt today. But this form of social banditry was an exclusive and private affair of Chinatown. Insofar as Chinatown's violent altercations were circumscribed not only by the invisible wall around the ghetto but also by the limited interests of the parties contending for women, wealth and power, the community was isolated by its internal conflicts. Whether manifested in fearful acquiescence or active participation, the ghetto's residents were bound together in a deadly kind of "antagonistic cooperation."

Since 1943 a progressive cycle of rebellion among Chinatown's youth has metamorphosed from crime to politics, from individual acts of aggression to collective acts of rebellion and from nonideological modes of hostility to the beginnings of a movement of ideological proportions. From 1943 until 1949 juvenile crime in Chinatown was largely the activity of a small number of native-born boys about 15 years of age, hurt by unemployment, difficulties in home life or inadequate income. Their crimes were typical of the most individualized and inarticulate forms of primitive rebellion. Burglary, auto theft, robberies, larcenies, hold-ups and assault and battery constituted 103 of the 184 offenses for which Chinese male juveniles were referred to San Francisco's juvenile court in those years. There were also gangs of native-born youth, apparently sponsored by or under the protection of secret societies, who occasionally assaulted and robbed strangers in Chinatown, not a few of whom, incidentally, were Japanese-Americans recently returned from wartime internment camps and also organized into clubs, cliques and gangs.

Petty criminal gangs emerged more frequently among both the native and foreign-born youth in Chinatown from 1958 to 1964. In some cases these gangs were composed of young men sponsored in their criminal activities by secret societies. An example was the "cat" burglary ring broken up by police in 1958 and discovered to be a branch of the Hop Sing Tong. Three years later, two gangs, the "Lums" and the "Rabble Rousers," were reported to be engaged in auto thefts, extortion, street fights and petty larcenies. In January 1964 members of a San Francisco Chinatown gang were charged with the $10,000 burglary of a fish market in suburban Mountain View. A year later, the police broke up the "Bugs," a youthful criminal gang whose members dressed entirely in black, with bouffant hair style and raised-heel boots, and who, in committing 48 burglaries, made off with $7,500 in cash and $3,000 in merchandise in a period of six months. The "Bugs"—who capitalized on an otherwise stigmatizing aspect of their existence, their short stature—reemerged a year later despite an attempt by Chinatown's leaders to quell juvenile gangs by bringing in street workers from San Francisco's Youth for Service to channel the gang toward constructive activities. By the mid-1960s Chinatown's burglary gangs had begun to branch out and were working areas of the city outside the Chinese quarter.

The present stage of a more politicized rebellion may be dated from the emergence in May 1967 of Leway, Incorporated. In its history up to August 1969, the Leways experienced almost precisely the pattern of problems and response that typically give rise first to nonideological rebellion and then, under certain conditions, to the development of revolutionary ideology. Leway (standing for "legitimate way") began as a public-spirited self-help group among American-born Chinese teen-agers. Aged 17 to 22, these young men organized to unite Chinatown's youth, to combat juvenile delinquency and to improve conditions in the poverty-stricken Chinese ghetto through helping youths to help themselves. In its first months it gained the support of such Chinatown luminaries as Lim P. Lee, now San Francisco's postmaster and a former probation officer, and other prominent citizens. Through raffles, loans and gifts, these youths, many of whom could be classed as delinquents, raised $2,000 to rent a pool hall near the Chinatown-Filipino border area. And, with the help of the Chinese YMCA and Youth for Service, they outfitted it with five pool tables, seven pinball machines, some chairs and a television set. "This is a hangout for hoods," said its president, Denny Lai, to reporter Ken Wong. "Most of us cats are misfits, outcasts with a rap sheet. What we're trying to do is to keep the hoods off the streets, give them something to do instead of raising hell."

Leway was a local indigenous group seeking to employ its own methods and style to solve its own members' problems. And it was precisely this that caused its downfall. Police refused to believe in methods that eschewed official surveillance, sporadic shakedowns and the not always occasional beating of a youth "resisting arrest." Leway tried a dialogue with the police, but it broke down over the rights of the latter to enter, search and seize members at Leway's headquarters, a tiny piece of "territory" which the young Chinese had hoped to preserve from alien and hostile intrusion. Leway claimed it wanted only to be left alone by this official arm of a society which they saw as already hostile. "We are not trying to bother them [the police] . . . and we won't go out of our way to work with them either."

In addition to continuous harassment by white police, Leway failed to establish its legitimacy in Chinatown itself. The Chinese Chamber of Commerce refused it official recognition, and as a result Leway could not gain access to the local Economic Opportunity Council to obtain much-needed jobs for Chinatown youth. The Tsung Tsin Association, which owned the building where Leway had its headquarters, threatened to raise the rent or lease the premises to another renter. Finally, whether rightly or not, the members of Leway, together with other Chinatown youth groups, were blamed for the increasing violence in Chinatown. Throughout 1968-69 reports of violent assault on tourists and rival gangs were coming out of Chinatown. Police stepped up their intrusive surveillance and other heavy-handed tactics. Chinese youth charged them with brutality, but the police replied that they were only using proper procedures in the line of a now more hazardous duty. In late summer 1969 the combination of police harassment, rent hikes, Leway's failure to secure jobs for its chronically unemployed members and its general inability to establish itself as a legitimate way of getting Chinatown youth "straightened out" took its final toll. Leway House closed its doors. Dreams of establishing on-the-job training for the unskilled, new business ventures for the unemployed, a pleasant soda fountain for Leway adolescents and an education and recreation program for Chinatown teen-agers—all this was smashed. The bitterness stung deep in the hearts of Chinatown young people. "Leway stood for legitimate ways," a 15-year-old youth told reporter Bill Moore. "Helluva lot of good it did them." The closing of Leway destroyed many Chinatown young people's faith in the official culture and its public representatives.

The stage was set for the next phase in the development of rebellion. Out of the shambles of Leway came the Red Guards, composed of the so-called radical elements of the former organization. But now Leway's search for legitimacy has been turned on its head. The Red Guards flaunt the little red book *Quotations from Chairman Mao Tse-tung* as their credo, make nonnegotiable demands on the power structure of Chinatown and the metropolis and openly espouse a program of disruption, rebellion and occasionally, it seems, revolution.

Leway had been modeled after other San Francisco youthful gang reform groups, but the Red Guards have adopted the organizational form, rhetorical style and political mood of the Black Panthers. A few years ago this would have seemed highly improbable. In the 1960s there were frequent bloody clashes between gangs of Chinese and Negroes, and interracial incidents at Samuel Gompers School—a kind of incarceration unit for black and Oriental incorrigibles—had not encouraged friendly relations among the two groups. Nevertheless it was just these contacts, combined with a growing awareness of Panther tactics and successes, and some not too secret proselytization by Panther leaders among the disaffected Leway members, that brought the young Chinese to adopt the black militant style. Whatever prejudices Chinese might harbor against Negroes, Black Panther rhetoric seemed perfectly to describe their own situation. After all, Leway had tried to be good, to play the game according to the white man's rules, and all it had gotten for its pains were a heap of abuse and a few cracked skulls. Now it was time to be realistic—"to stop jiving" and "to tell it like it is." Police were "pigs"; white men were "honkies"; officially developed reform programs were attempts to "shine" on credulous Chinese youth; and the goal to be attained was not integration, not material success, but power. "We're an organization made up mainly of street people and we're tired of asking the government for reforms," said Alex Hing, a 23-year-old Chinese who is the minister of information of the Red Guards. "We're going to attain power, so we don't have to beg any more."

The Red Guards are a populist group among Chinatown's "primitive" rebels. They stand against not one but two power structures in their opposition to oppression and poverty—that of old Chinatown and that of the larger metropolis. Ideologically they are located somewhere between the inarticulate rumblings of rustic rebels and the full-scale ideology of unregenerate revolutionaries. They cry out for vengeance against the vague but powerful complex of Chinese and white elites that oppress them. They dream of a world in which they will have sufficient power to curb their exploiters' excesses; meanwhile they do the best they can to right local wrongs and to ingratiate themselves with the mass of their Chinatown compatriots. The free breakfasts for indigent youngsters, a copy of the Panthers' program, attracts popular support among Chinatown's poor at the same time that it shames Chinatown's elites for allowing the community's children to go hungry. The demand for the release of all imprisoned Asians seems to place the Red Guards squarely on the side of all those "little people" of Chinatown who feel themselves victimized by an alien and oppressive police system. However, their ethnic consciousness usually supersedes and sometimes clashes with their alleged attachment to a class-oriented ideology, as it did when the Red Guards accepted an invitation to guard a meeting of the Chinese Garment

Contractors' Association against a threatened assault by Teamsters seeking to organize Chinatown's heavily exploited dressmakers. But it is precisely their parochial dedication to a sense of Chinese ethnicity that endears them to the less hardy of young Chinatowners who secretly share their dilemmas and dreams, as well as limits their political effectiveness.

Populist rebellion is not the only form of social politics in Chinatown. A conservative type of rebelliousness is illustrated in the evolution of the Hwa Ching and the Junior Hwa Ching. Hwa Ching emerged in 1967 as a loose association of mostly Hong Kong-born youth in Chinatown. Estimates of its size vary from 25 to 300, and this fact alone testifies to its low degree of cohesiveness and the sense of drift that characterizes its members. Until very recently Hwa Ching was represented in most public discussions by a "spokesman" (its looseness of organization prevented any greater clarification of title), George Woo, a former photographer who took on the task of bridging the communication gap between the largely Chinese-speaking youths and the officials of the metropolis. The aims of this association are difficult to ascertain exactly, partly because there was little agreement among its members and partly because spokesman Woo usually tended to a violently polemical speaking style in order to call attention to the situation of Chinatown's immigrants. Hwa Ching had less of a perfected program than a set of practical problems. Hong Kong youth were insufficiently educated and skilled to obtain any jobs other than Chinatown's dreary positions of waiter, busboy and sweated laborer; unequipped linguistically to enter the metropolis and, in the beginning, unwilling to accept confinement in a congested, poverty-stricken and despotically ruled ghetto.

Hwa Ching seemed to form itself around El Piccolo, an espresso coffeehouse opened in Chinatown in 1967 and operated by Dick and Alice Barkley. Alice Barkley, herself a Hong Kong-born Chinese, turned the coffeehouse into a haven for foreign-born Chinese youth. There they could meet in peace and with freedom to discuss, argue, complain and occasionally plan some joint activity. Reaction to their clubby fraternization at El Piccolo was mixed. Traditional Chinatowners accused the Barkleys of offering asylum to raffish criminal elements; a newly aroused college and university group of Chinese-Americans praised the establishment of a place for impoverished immigrants to congregate; and most San Franciscans didn't even know the Hwa Ching existed.

Early in 1968 Hwa Ching approached the Human Relations Commission, the Economic Development Council and the Chinese business elite to ask for their aid in establishing an educational program for alleviating the misery of Chinatown's immigrant youth. Their approach was unusually frank and plainly practical. They proposed the establishment of a comprehensive two-year educational program to provide Chinatown's young immigrants with a high school diploma and vocational training in auto repair, business machine operation, construction, sheet metal, electrical installation and plumbing. They closed with a statement that was unfortunately taken as a warning and a threat. "We've been hearing too many promises. The rise and fall of our hopes is tragic and ominous."

This first bid for help was unsuccessful. In late February, however, the Hwa Ching tried again and spoke to the Chinatown Advisory Board of the Human Relations Commission. This time Hwa Ching, represented by the fiery George Woo, was more modest in its request for a comprehensive program, but more militant in its presentation. Hwa Ching wanted $4,322 to build a clubhouse, but although Woo reiterated the same arguments as other Hwa Chings had presented in January, the tone was different.

Describing his constituents, Woo said, "There is a hard core of delinquents in Chinatown who came from China. Their problems are the problems of all poor with the addition that they don't speak English." Then he added that "they're talking about getting guns and rioting. . . . I'm not threatening riots. The situation already exists, but if people in Chinatown don't feel threatened they won't do anything about it." The mention of guns and the warning of possible riots were too much for John Yehall Chin, a prominent Chinese businessman, principal of Saint Mary's Chinese Language School and member of the Human Relations Commission's Chinatown Advisory Board. In reply to the Hwa Ching's request he advised the commission, and indirectly the youths, "They have not shown that they are sorry or that they will change their ways. They have threatened the community. If you give in to this group, you are only going to have another hundred immigrants come in and have a whole new series of threats and demands." Although the commission expressed its interest, Hwa Ching's demand was rejected.

They tried again. In March the Hwa Ching's president, Stan Wong, presented the immigrant youths' case before the Chinese Six Companies, the oligarchy that controls Chinatown. Speaking in Cantonese, Wong repudiated the threat of riots made at the February meeting. "We made no threats," he said. "They were made by nonmembers. We need to help ourselves. We look to the future and are mindful of the immigrant youths who will be coming here later. We hope they do not have to go through what we've been through." Later he answered a question about possible Communist affiliation: "Hwa Ching is not involved with any political ideology." Although Commissioner Chin pointed out that the Hwa Ching had mended its ways, the Six Companies refused them help. Meanwhile the Human Relations Commission, under the direction of Chin, organized an Establishment-controlled Citizens for Youth in Chinatown. The Hwa Ching felt utterly rejected.

In their bitterness and anger, however, the Hwa Ching did not turn to populist revolt, as had the Leways. Instead they fragmented even more. Their loose coalition at El Piccolo ended when that establishment closed its doors in August 1968. The Hwa Ching had never in fact professed an ideology. What seemed to be one was more a product of the fervid imaginations of alarmed whites and of the fiery invective of George Woo than it was any coherent line of political or revolutionary thought. The Hwa Ching's practical needs were too immediate, their literacy in English too low and their limited but practical political experience in Hong Kong and Chinatown too real for them to accept an organization that used Mao's red book and which therefore ran for them the risks of political persecution and possible deportation. As Tom Tom, a 23-year-old immigrant who had been one of the earliest members of Hwa Ching, explained to a reporter, the immigrant youth were independent of the Leway and all other Chinatown groups, affected none of the hippie-Che-Raoul-Panther styles and wanted little more than jobs, girls and to be left alone. The Hwa Ching found themselves oppressed by their supposed allies nearly as much as by their condition. Leways boys and other American-born Chinese called them "Chinabugs" and attacked them in gang rumbles; Negroes picked on the dimunitive Chinese until they learned to retaliate in numbers and with tactics; college students sought to tutor and to evangelize them with secular and sometimes political ideas but succeeded mostly in making them feel inferior and frightened by a kind of politics they abhorred.

By the middle of 1969 the Hwa Ching had split into three factions. One returned to the streets to fight, burglarize and assault all those available symbols and representatives of the seemingly monolithic power structure that had scorned them; two other factions apparently accepted co-optation into Chinatowns's two most powerful though age-ridden secret societies—the Suey Sing and Hop Sing Tongs. There their anger could find outlet at the same time that their strength could be utilized for traditional aims. The secret societies could pay for the immigrant youths' basic needs and with the same expenditure buy the muscle to keep control of their own interests and institutions. And since the Tongs were part of the complex congeries of associations that make up Chinatowns's power elite, it is not surprising that leaders of this same elite gave tacit approval to the Tongs' recruitment of what had appeared in early 1968 to be a serious threat to the old order. Unlike the Leway, which could not join the old order and may have been too Americanized to accept secret society patronage, the immigrant youth find in it a perhaps temporary expedient in their dilemma. Not being politicized, they can more readily join in the protection of old Chinatown. They have resumed a posture typical of earlier youthful generations' response to anger and poverty in Chinatown. They form the conservative wing of Chinatown's complex structure of conflict and rebellion.

In other areas and times of primitive rebellion, conservative and populist factions often fought each other as much as their professed enemies. Similarly, in Chinatown the young toughs who have become paid guards of the secret societies' and, occasionally, the Six Companies' meetings are not infrequently arrayed against the Leway—Red Guard gangs. And in this sense young Chinatown recapitulates a structure of conflict that characterized that of its earlier generations. Conservative-populist conflicts isolate the contending parties from outside groups and larger issues. The violent fights and smouldering feuds appear to noncomprehending outsiders to be exclusively Chinese in their nature and content. And this intramural conflict in turn circumscribes Chinatown and once again cuts it off from the metropolis.

However, connections to the larger society of San Francisco in particular and the United States in general do exist. For the youth the most important one is the Intercollegiate Chinese for Social Action (ICSA). This group was formed at San Francisco State College from among the more socially concerned and politically aware Chinese-American students. For a while it managed the special program by which Chinese students from the ghetto were recruited to the college. But the long Third World strike at San Francisco State College in 1968-69 radicalized its members and propelled them into even greater contact with the Chinatown community. They became actively oriented toward conditions about which they had been only vaguely aware before. ICSA asserted aloud and with emphasis what had been but an open secret for decades—Chinatown was a racial ghetto—poverty-stricken, disease-ridden, overcrowded, underdeveloped and with a population growing in Malthusian proportions. To the remedy of all these defects they dedicated themselves and established offices not only in the college but in Chinatown itself. ICSA provides tutoring services to Chinatown's less educated youth and urges that San Francisco State College establish even more programs for community rehabilitation. The community-oriented Chinese college youth do not openly attack Leway or the Red Guards but remain in communication with them as well as with the erstwhile Hwa Ching. But, observes George Woo, now as an ICSA member, "We can also see the pitfalls in using too much of the blarney, as the Red Guards did. As a result, they alienated immigrant youths and the whole community in three months' time." By keeping open contacts among the native- and the foreign-born, among Hwa Ching and Leway-Red Guards, among status conscious diploma-bearers and socially stigmatized delinquents and among the legitimated and the lowly, ICSA may yet be able to blunt the deadly edge of conflict and build a durable community for Chinatown.

What this means specifically is by no means clear even to the ICSA members themselves. "I'm still trying to figure out what I am supposed to be as a Chinese-American," complained a 21-year-old college student, echoing the inner nagging question of most of his compatriots. And George Woo replied, "I know how you feel. I don't identify with China either and I certainly don't identify with the petty American middle-class values of my aunts and uncles." ICSA emphasizes a two-way learning process between the lettered and the dropouts and calls for the formulation of a new ethic to replace the Confucian-Protestant ethos of Chinese America. As ICSA leader Mason Wong has said, "Our generation here will no longer accept the old and still prevalent Confucian doctrine of success coming only from hard work and humility." What that ethic will be is not yet known. However, the Chinese must still contend with the traditional social order that is Chinatown's Establishment.

Anyone at all conversant with San Francisco's Chinatown will have heard of the Chinese Six Companies. In a vague sense he might know about some of its activities, be able to point out its headquarters and note that it is a benevolent, protective and representational body of Chinese who enjoy unofficial but influential standing at City Hall. Beyond this he might know very little but the familiar litany that the Chinese take care of themselves, contribute little, if at all, to the welfare rolls or to the city's alarming rate of juvenile delinquency and that, while the Chinese were perhaps at one time a troublesome minority, they are now safely ensconced in their own quarter of the city where they enjoy a modicum of freedom to practice peculiar cultural expressions derived from a China that is no more. To him the Six Companies is one aspect of that cultural freedom.

Like many stereotypes that arise in racist societies, this one too contains some kernels of truth. The Chinese in San Francisco, like the Chinese in Calcutta, Singapore, Bangkok, Saigon, Manila and indeed in almost every large city to which Chinese have migrated, enjoy a measure of home rule that far exceeds that of any other minority group in the metropolis. During the colonial period in Southeast Asia, the British and Dutch formalized their practices of indirect rule into a specified system of titles. "Kapitan China" was the Dutch designation for the uniformed and bemedalled Chinese who represented his people in the colonial councils at Batavia, and the "Captain China" system prevailed in British Malaya and other colonies as well. For the colonial powers indirect rule was an expedient way of maintaining sufficient control over restless and hostile native peoples in a precariously pluralistic society in order to extract their labor and the colony's natural resources without having to contend with all their tribal and customary ways and woes. For the subject peoples it meant that they could freely organize their lives in accordance with traditional practices, so long as they didn't interfere with the rather limited interests of the imperial powers. Outside the colonial area, Chinese immigrant elites also managed to establish a kind of cultural extraterritoriality and to achieve an added legitimation to their traditional control over their fellow migrants by winning unofficial but practically useful recognition from white civic elites. In Vancouver, and in New York City the Chinese Benevolent Association has obtained such perogatives; in San Francisco it is the Chinese Six Companies.

But to understand Chinatown's power structure fully, it is necessary to analyze the several kinds of traditional associations from which it is composed. First there are clan associations, or "family associations" as Occidental journalist and sociologist usually term them. Clan associations derive from the lineage communities so prevalent in Kwangtung and ideally unite all persons descended from a common male ancestor. Overseas, however, the more manageable lineage unit was replaced by a kinship network wider than that which originally enclosed only a compact village. The clan association includes all who bear the same surname. In the early days of Chinese immigration, the clan associations became a special kind of immigrant aid society providing the newcomer with food, shelter, employment, protection and advice. Furthermore, the clan leaders reminded the immigrant of his obligations to parents and family in the home village and, in the absence of the village elders, assumed a role in loco parentis, settling disputes, arbitrating disagreements and in general containing intraclan differences within the kinship fold. Some clan associations exercised a monopoly over a trade or profession in Chinatown and effectively resisted encroachments on these monopolies by ambitious Chinese upstarts from other clans. Until the recent arrival of large numbers of immigrants from Hong Kong, the clan associations had been declining in power and authority as a result of the aging of their members and the acculturation of the American-born Chinese. However, even this new lifeblood is less acquiescent than the former sojourner members. Chinatown clan associations are now challenged to provide something more than a paltry benevolence in exchange for their petty despotism.

In addition to clans, however, there developed among overseas Chinese a functionally similar but structurally different type of association. The *hui kuan* united all those who spoke a common dialect, hailed from the same district in China or belonged to the same tribal or ethnic group. (It is a mistake to suppose, as many Occidentals do, that the peoples of China are culturally homogeneous. In the tiny area around Canton from which most of America's immigrants have come, there are numerous dialects which, while they have a common script, are almost mutually unintelligible when spoken.) In many ways the hui kuan were similar to those immigrant aid and benevolent societies established by Germans, Irish, Jews and other Europeans in America. In San Francisco and other cities in which Chinese dwelt, the hui kuan, like the clan association, maintained a headquarters and served as caravansary, hostelry, credit association and employment agency. In all these matters it exercised authoritarian control, and since most of the Chinese in America were debtors, directly or indirectly, to their hui kuan, its officers were not infrequently suspected of taking an excessive interest or a corrupt profit from their charges. The hui kuan, again similar to the clan, conducted arbitration and mediation hearings between disputing members, managed and collected the debts of its members and in addition charged them various fees for its services. An aging membership and the flight of the American-born bourgeoisie tended to undermine hui kuan authority, but the old businesses in Chinatown still affiliate with them and accept their mediation and arbitration services. They are especially important in the ownership and control of Chinatown property which they administer in a traditional way quite different from real estate management in the Occidental parts of the city.

The third major type of association in Chinatown is the secret society. Like the clan and the hui kuan, the secret society originated in China where for centuries it served as a principal agency for popular protest, violent rebellion and social banditry. The overseas migrants from Kwangtung included not a few members of the Triad Society, the most famous of China's clandestine associations. In nearly every significant overseas community of Chinese they established chapters of, or models based on that order. In the United States secret societies among the Chinese were set up by the early immigrants in the cities and also in those outlying areas where clans and hui kuan could not form a solid base. Inside Chinatown the secret societies soon took over control of gambling and prostitution, and it is with these activities rather than with their political or charitable activities that they are most often associated in the minds of non-Chinese in America. Clans, hui kuan and the several chapters of secret societies often fell out with one another over their competition for women, wealth and power inside Chinatown, and these so-called tong wars raged intermittently until a Chinatown Peace Association established a still perilous peace between the warring factions in the 1920s. The charitable works of secret societies were confined for the most part to giving mutual aid to their own members, the establishment of headquarters and hostelries and in recent years the building of clubhouses where their aged bachelor members might find hospitable fraternity. The political activities of the secret societies have consisted in their intermittent interest in the fortunes of China's several regimes, but they have not shown any particular interest in upsetting the national politics of the United States. Meanwhile the seret societies' most successful source of revenue in Chinatown—the control over gambling and prostitution—diminished as the Chinese bachelors aged and died and the American-born declined interest in these activities. The recruitment of the newly arrived and disaffected immigrant youth from Chinatown has undoubtedly done much to rejuvenate these societies, but it remains to be seen whether this will lengthen their life as institutions in America or change their function in accordance with new interests and current developments.

At the top of the community power structure of Chinatown is the Chinese Benevolent Association, commonly
known as the Chinese Six Companies. It was formed in the
late 1850s as a confederation of hui kuan—later it incorporated clans, guilds and, reluctantly, secret societies
—in order to provide communitywide governance, to promote intracommunity harmony and to present at least the
appearance of a common Chinese front to white society.
Until the 1870s it functioned as an agency of international diplomacy and consular activity as well, since the
Chinese Empire did not provide a specific overseas office
for those duties. The Six Companies has been the principal spokesman for the Chinese to white America. It has
protested against anti-Chinese legislation, helped fight
discriminatory laws in the courts, petitioned federal, state
and local governments in behalf of the Chinese and generally provided Chinatown with a modest respectability in
the face of sinophobic stereotypy. One of its more recent
efforts in defense of Chinese in America was a protest
against Secretary of Transportation John Volpe's omission
of the role that Chinese played in the building of the Trans-
continental Railroad when he spoke at the centenary celebration of its completion.

Gradually the Six Companies established its legitimacy
as rightful representatives of the Chinese in San Francisco.
Composed of merchants and traders, the leaders of the Six
Companies seemed to inspire assurance among civic leaders that the Chinese were not a threat to the city's economic
base. Moreover, the anti-Chinese movement in America
was largely a movement of small farmers and laborers
against what they described as the unfair competition of
Chinese laborers. Once labor agitation had succeeded in
driving the Chinese workers out of the city's industries and
into the confines of Chinatown—a mission largely accomplished by 1910—civic functionaries were quite pre-

pared to negotiate with the Six Companies whatever agreements might have to be reached between the ghetto and the metropolis. For its part the Six Companies, although it protested against the excesses of ghettoization, must have realized the gain to be made in its own power by having the great majority of Chinese housed and employed in Chinatown. The final establishment of Chinatown as an unofficial but real quarter of the city consolidated and enhanced the power of the Six Companies over its denizens.

In effect the Six Companies' authority over Chinese in San Francisco was—until the advent of the American-born and the rise of intracommunity rebellion—an institutionalized version of the kind of control over Negroes in America exercised by Booker T. Washington and his "Tuskegee Machine" from 1890 until 1915. The slow growth of a second generation prevented an effective counteraction to its powers by an acculturated group demanding a new politics. To be sure, Chinatown's Six Companies had its W. E. B. DuBoises—men who opposed the despotic benevolence it exercised, the containment of Chinese in the ghetto that it tacitly espoused and the corruption in its offices. But they were too few in number to be effective, too readily co-opted into the controlled violence of Chinatown's secret societies or too easily frightened into silence by threats of financial loss, deportation or conviction of trumped-up crimes in the white man's courts, where Chinese interpreters could be bought and perjured witnesses were easily obtainable. When the American-born generation did reach maturity, many of its members went to college, entered the professions and departed from Chinatown. This caused the Six Companies some loss in its Chinese constituency, but, since the Chinese-Americans *embourgeoisés* did not challenge the authority of the Six Companies, the loss did not undermine its control over Chinatown.

Today, in addition to the "illegitimate" rebellion of youth in Chinatown, there is a "legitimate" counteraction of adults against the communitywide authority of the Six Companies. This loyal opposition includes several intra-Chinatown associations composed of "respectable" members of the American-born and, occasionally, a foreign-born Chinese leader who opposes the associational oligarchy. Until 1956 the only significant organization among the American-born Chinese was the Chinese-American Citizens' Alliance, a group so small that in its early days, more than a half century ago, it was little more than a name promising assimilation. Since the mid-1950s, however, a new association has arisen—the Chinese-American Democratic Club (CADC). This organization of politically minded and socially conscious Chinese-Americans heralds a shift from communal-oriented traditionalism to civic-minded cosmopolitanism in Chinatown. Still another organization outside the domination of the Six Companies is the Concerned Chinese for Action and Change, a loose and informal association of middle-class Chinese-Americans who live outside the ghetto but who can be counted on to mass for support of more liberal social action in Chinatown. Third, the Chinatown-North Beach Area Youth Council, a product of the Economic Development Agency in Chinatown, seeks to link up the respectable middle-class Chinatowners with its less respectable youth groups. Finally, there is one aging Chinese, J. K. Choy, who almost alone has opposed the old order in Chinatown without effective reprisal. A Columbia-educated banker and a professed disciple of Fabianism, Choy has exposed the poverty and neglect hidden beneath the tinseled glitter of Chinatown's neon-lit ghetto. He organized a reading room and English classes for immigrants in the offices next to the branch bank which he oversees as general manager. When in October 1966 he advised the women employed in

Chinatown's sweatshops to organize for better wages, shorter hours and improved conditions and offered a devastating criticism of the ghetto's poverty program, rumors were started in the community which resulted in a three-day run on the bank. Unlike the old Chinese boycotts, which were used so effectively in the early days of the economically isolated Chinatown, this attempt to destroy a Chinatown reformer failed because the bank was protected by its connections to the larger banking system of the state. The failure to silence Choy by traditional methods is a measure of the ghetto's growing interdependence with the nation and a testimony to the decreasing power of traditional sanctions available to intracommunity elites.

In Chinatown the arena of battle between the new opposition and the old order has been for seats on the poverty board organized under the community action program of the Economic Opportunity Act of 1964. In April 1969, after three years of internicine infighting, the liberal opposition—largely composed of the members of the CADC—was finally able to depose the Six Companies' man on the board, Chairman Dapien Liang, and to replace him with a chairman more to its liking. The Six Companies charged that the poverty board was dominated by "left-wing militants" but was unable to secure its complete control over Chinatown's poverty program. However, the Chinatown program is budgeted so far only to the beginning of 1970. If the program is scrapped, the arena of conflict and opposition in Chinatown may shift on to some other plane.

Another challenge to the old order has been hurled recently by ICSA. In August 1969 a news reporter interviewed Foo Hum, tea merchant, mogul in the Chinese Six Companies and representative on the Chinatown antipoverty board, concerning Chinatown's social problems. In addition to denying that the community's problems were either exclusive or very grave, Hum refuted the assertion that they were attributable to newly arrived immigrants. Then he launched into an attack on the native-born youth, especially the Red Guards and the ICSA and was quoted in the press as saying, "The Red Guards and the Intercollegiate Chinese for Social Action—theirs are Communist activities. They should not be blamed on the new immigrants." ICSA promptly filed a slander suit against Hum for $100,000 general damages and $10,000 punitive damages. Hum, backed by a Six Companies legal defense fund of $10,000, refused to settle out of court to an offer made by Mason Wong, ICSA president, that the suit be dropped in return for Hum's writing a letter of apology and publishing it in all local papers, paying all legal fees that have arisen thus far and donating a token gift of money to ICSA.

The crust of Chinatown's cake of customary control may be beginning to crumble. The old order must contend not only with the mounting opposition of the community's respectable, professional and American-born younger and middle-aged adults, but also with the militant organization of Chinatown's disaffected youth. In addition, one cannot count on the new immigrants to bow to Chinatown's traditional power elite in the future as they have in the past.

It is by no means clear, however, what the outcome of this continuing power struggle will be. Chinatown's more liberal-minded leaders may defeat themselves by their ambiguous support of both progressive policies and a new racial consciousness. The former may call for a need to push for the introduction of unionization and other characteristic features of white America into Chinatown's anachronistic institutions. But the new ethnic consciousness, a consciousness that in its extreme forms opposes both the old order of transplanted Cathay and the middle-class ways of white America, may forbid cooperation with those institutions—progressive or not—that are dominated by Caucasians. It is in this possible paralysis that Chinatown's old order coalesces with its new rebels. Both seem to oppose the imposition of the metropolis upon the ghetto, but for quite different reasons. For the old elites any greater instrusion might undermine their exclusive and "extraterritorial" power; for the new rebels any intrusion might wrest away their newly discovered desire for ethnic self-determination. It would not be impossible for Chinatown's garment workers, as well as the community's other unprotected and impoverished denizens, to be caught helplessly in the vice of this excruciating cultural conflict.

Beyond the problems of the ghetto itself—some of which are typical of all poor ethnic enclaves in American cities, some of which are peculiarly Chinese—loom the attitude and action of the larger society. Chinatown's myth of social propriety, communal self-help, familial solidarity and a low crime rate was a carefully nurtured mystique, prepared to counteract the vicious stereotype of coolie laborers, immoral practices, murderous tong wars and inscrutable cunning that characterized the American white man's perspective. As a pervasive mystique coloring most reports of Chinatown for the past three decades, it has succeeded up to a point in its original purpose—to substitute a favorable stereotype for an unfavorable one. It had other latent functions as well, not the least of which was to protect the community's social and political structure from excessive scrutiny and destruction. So long as Chinatown could "contain" its problems, circumscribe its paragovernmental institutions with bourgeois or innocuously exotic descriptions and control its members, the community was safe, and the city adopted a relaxed attitude toward its own cosmopolitan character.

But Chinatown's safety rests also on America's foreign relations with China. The repeal of the exclusion laws in 1943 was a gesture of reconciliation toward the country's wartime ally in the war against Japan, just as the incarceration of the Japanese-Americans during that same war was a hostile move against those Americans who had the misfortune to be physically identifiable with America's enemy. Aware of the dangerously changeable character of America's friendliness toward her racially visible peoples, Chinatown has presented a picture of cultural identity with nineteenth-century Cathay and of moral sympathy for the Nationalist Regime in Taiwan. This is not a false picture, for the political identity of the aged aliens is of very low intensity, but if it must be linked to old China it is most probably to the Republic founded by Sun Yat Sen and continued under Chiang Kai-shek. The American-born Chinese are not "Zionists" to any degree and therefore feel themselves to be Americans politically and socially and do not identify with either China. Even the Red Guard's rhetorical usage of Mao's book is more a symbol of an American rebellion than the substance of Communist affiliation. And the new immigrants have shown a profound disinterest in associating even with the symbols of Maoism.

Nevertheless, the fires of fear and prejudice are still kindled in America. Not only are acts of prejudice and discrimination still visited upon Chinese-Americans in everyday life, at least one agency of the government itself is still not wholly satisfied with the loyalty of Chinese in America. On April 17, 1969 J. Edgar Hoover testified before a subcommittee of the House Committee on Appropriations that "the blatant, belligerent and illogical statements made by Red China's spokesmen during the past year leave no doubt that the United States is Communist China's No. 1 enemy." Hoover went on to warn the subcommittee of Communist Chinese intelligence activity "overt and covert, to obtain needed material, particularly in the scientific field." After hinting darkly that a Chinese-American who served a 60-day sentence in prison for making a false customs declaration about electronic parts being sent to Hong Kong might have been an agent of a Communist country, Hoover asserted, "We are being confronted with a growing amount of work in being alert for Chinese Americans and others in this country who would assist Red China in supplying needed material or promoting Red Chinese propaganda." "For one thing," he continued, "Red China has been flooding the country with its propaganda and there are over 300,000 Chinese in the United States, some of whom could be susceptible to recruitment either through ethnic ties or hostage situations because of relatives in Communist China." Hoover went on to say that "up to 20,000 Chinese immigrants can come into the United States each year and this provides a means to send illegal agents into our Nation." Hoover concluded his testimony on this point by asserting that "there are active Chinese Communist sympathizers in the Western Hemisphere in a position to aid in operations against the United States." Thus the Chinese in America were reminded that perhaps all their efforts at convincing white America that they were a peaceable, law-abiding, family-minded and docile people who contributed much and asked little in return had gone for naught. In time of crisis they too might suffer the same fate that overtook the highly acculturated Japanese-Americans a quarter century before—wholesale incarceration. When Hoover's remarks are coupled with the widespread report in 1966 that China's atomic bomb was "fathered" by Dr. Tsien Hwue-shen, an American-educated Chinese who was persecuted here for five years during the McCarthy era and then allowed to return to the country of his birth and citizenship, and with the fact that under Title II of the Emergency Detention Act of 1950 any person or group who is deemed to be a "threat to the internal security of the United States" may be incarcerated in the same detention camps in which the American Japanese were imprisoned, the safety of the Chinese in America from official persecution is by no means assured. The Chinese, of course, protested against Hoover's remarks, and one San Francisco paper labeled his testimony an irresponsible slur on "a large and substantial segment of American citizens." Meanwhile, Japanese-American, Chinese-American and several other kinds of organizations have joined together to attempt to get Congress to repeal the infamous Title II.

Race prejudice, as Herbert Blumer has reminded us, is a sense of group position. It arises out of the belief, supported and legitimated by various elites, that a racial group is both inferior and threatening. Such a belief may lie dormant beneath the facade of a long-term racial accommodation, made benign by a minority group's tacit agreement to live behind the invisible, but no less real for that, wall of a ghetto. Then when circumstances seem to call for new meanings and different explanations, the allegedly evil picture and supposedly threatening posture may be resuscitated to account for political difficulties or social problems that seem to defy explanation.

History, however, does not simply repeat itself. There is a new Chinatown and new sorts of Chinese in America. The old order holds its power precariously in the ghetto, and the new liberals and the now vocal radicals bid fair to supplant them and try new solutions to the old problems. Finally, the Japanese experience of 1942 may not be repeated either because the United States has learned that lesson too well or because too many Americans would not let it happen again.

The Game of Black and White at Hunters Point

ARTHUR E. HIPPLER

Hunters Point is a depressed and isolated district in the southeastern section of San Francisco. It is adjacent to the Hunters Point naval shipyard where some of the residents work. Generally, though, unemployment is widespread. There are still people living in shanty dwellings erected as "temporary" housing during World War II. Housing in general is inadequate or substandard, and the whole district is defined by the City Housing Authority as an official low-income area. Many, if not most, of the residents draw some form of public assistance. Nearly all of them are black. Less notorious than Oakland, on the other side of the Bay, the district is usually ignored until some act of violence or a crusading newspaperman brings it to public attention. Casual violence is certainly prevalent; so are prostitution and narcotics-dealing. It is a true ghetto, despised and neglected as far as possible by the rest of the city. Its votes have been taken for granted by the Democrats, ignored by the Republicans. It is poorly serviced;

53

garbage collection is irregular; public transport is inadequate. Hunters Pointers are clearly an outcast community in San Francisco.

In September 1966 rioting broke out there after a black teenager named Matthew Johnson had been shot dead by a white policeman while running away from a car that he and two friends had abandoned. The policeman (also named Johnson) suspected the car to be stolen and had failed to get the boy to stop. The disturbance which followed lasted for five days. I was doing participant field work in the area both before and after these events; Hunters Point is, I think, one of the few communities involved in the series of urban disturbances of the sixties to have engaged the attentions of such a researcher at such a time. While I cannot propose solutions, I hope I can help to clarify the complex interaction out of which such disturbances grow, and particularly to show some of the ways in which urban blacks and whites perceive themselves and each other and how these perceptions determine relations between them.

This project, nicknamed the Free Fuse, was founded in 1968 by Dr. Roger Smith, director of the Amphetamine Research Project housed in the clinic, and by a Lutheran minister in his mid-thirties named John Frykman. Financed by personal gifts and by grants from such private foundations as the Merrill Trust, its goal is to wean drug-abusers away from their destructive life-style. Using methods developed by Synanon and the Esalen Institute, Frykman and the other Free Fuse counselors have attempted to create a close and productive social unit out of alienated adolescents living together as the clinic's second communal family. They have also provided educational and employment opportunities for more than 500 young people in the past one and a half years.

Since many Free Fuse graduates are still involved in his

project, Frykman has also found it possible to expand. Having recently opened an annex in the drug-ridden North Beach District under the supervision of a psychiatric nurse, he has allowed the Drug Treatment Program to geographically qualify for inclusion in the Northeast Mental Health Center, a cachtment area encompassing one-quarter of San Francisco. Because of this, the Free Fuse will participate in a substantial grant from the National Institute of Mental Health being administered by Dr. Carfagni. Frykman's Drug Treatment Program has already received some of these funds, and he is therefore making arrangements with the downtown YMCA to open a similar center in the city's Tenderloin area. "We've never gotten a penny from any public agency before," he says, "but the future looks bright from here."

This optimism certainly seems justified, and Frykman is not the only staff member who insists that the clinic is in better shape than at any other point in its history. Yet, as indicated earlier, the facility has problems all the same. In the first place, although the volunteers working at 409 and 558 Clayton Street can point to their share of therapeutic successes, they cannot really help most of the individuals who now live in the Haight-Ashbury. Many of the volunteers are actually former patients; some of them can keep off drugs only if they are kept on the staff.

Second, and most important, is the fact that the Haight continues to deteriorate in spite of the clinic's efforts. Thus, the relatively healthy adolescents tend to abandon the district, leaving behind their more disturbed counterparts, as well as the older individuals who preceded them in the area. Because of this, some staff members at the Medical and Psychological Sections believe that the clinic has outlived its usefulness in its present form. Others argue that the facility should address itself to the problems not only of the new population but of the old community as well. Dr.

Matzger will probably have an important voice in this matter, and although his study might prompt the United States Public Health Service to support the work at 409 and 558 Clayton Street, it may mean a radical transformation in these centers as they now stand. This is a distinct possibility, for the clinic's future, like its past, is intimately connected with the district it serves.

To fully appreciate this it is necessary to visualize the Haight in 1960, before its present population arrived. In that year, rising rents, police harassment and the throngs of tourists and thrill-seekers on Grant Avenue squeezed many beatniks out of the North Beach District three miles away. They started looking for space in the Haight-Ashbury, and landlords here saw they could make more money renting their property to young people willing to put up with poor conditions than to black families. For this reason, a small, beat subculture took root in the Flatlands and spread slowly up the slope of Mount Sutro. By 1962 the Haight was the center of a significant but relatively unpublicized bohemian colony.

Social scientists have described at length the personal and social disorders among black Americans and have attributed them to centuries of subjugation by whites. Demands made of them both before and since the abolition of slavery have created, through the enforced absence of the male, a matrifocal family structure. Because of this, it is held, black males have strong but unconscious feelings of ineffectuality and castration, while women have to cope with fears of desertion by their men. These fears are realistic enough in Hunters Point, where 50 to 80 percent of families have no resident male. The women protect themselves by showing aggressive independence, and the men, attacked as potential nonproviders and deserters, often defend themselves—and open the way to welfare grants for their children—by actually abandoning their families. Moreover, these insecurities are intensified by internalized self-contempt. Blacks despise themselves because for years they have been despised by whites. The black American situation is a vicious cycle. Bad education is caused both by a realistic indifference to scholarly achievement and by expectations that blacks will fail— expectations built into the school system and the minds of its personnel, many of whom are poor teachers and nearly all of whom are white. Bad education (and lack of motivation) itself contributes to a low income level. Since white domination has forced acceptance of the consumer ethic on blacks, they are further frustrated by not having access to the material goods which validate that ethic.

Individuals growing up against such a background face continual evidence of their infantile status in white eyes but have no certain status of their own to grasp as an alternative. Many therefore take an image of themselves which derives in part from their own defensive psychological needs and in part from the fantasies of whites: the image of the hypersexual, hyperaggressive "Bad Nigger." In this way they can support themselves against recognizing how passive they are—"I'm a *bad* mother-fucker." Alternatively, they may repress emotion—"Man, I don't feel nothing"—or show covert and overt concerns about sexual potency. These stances all help to buttress their precarious image of themselves. The blacks of Hunters Point have menial jobs in a white world. They see the police, the guardians of that world, as "enemies." Such internal organization that exists is dominated by middle-aged matriarchs. The young can be expected to respond to all this in several ways. Passivity, bravado and explosive reaction are three stages of response, but elements of all three can be seen in any one. Passivity can be a revolt, bravado gives only the form of manliness, and explosive violence is rarely organized. In the case of Hunters Point, the violence included the first two elements as well.

The Hunters Point resident police are Housing Authority police. They do not belong to the San Francisco Police Department and, being essentially private police, they are theoretically limited in what laws they may enforce and where. They have the same right of arrest as any private citizen. Though their captain is a municipal police force inspector assigned to the Potrero Hill Station, San Francisco police rarely entered Hunters Point before the riot.

The Housing Authority police actually seem to function as a buffer between Hunters Point residents and adequate police protection. Indeed, the residents complain bitterly, not of the brutality of the racially integrated Housing Authority police, but of their refusal to give meaningful police protection. The tenants point out that the main job of the police seems to be to let people into their houses (after they have inadvertently locked themselves out) for a five dollar fee.

□ Them kids come into the halls shootin' them craps and turnin' over the fire extinguishers, and you call the cops and they tell you, "Don't worry they's just kids." I used to walk from the bus stop in 1946, and up to 1950, but I haven't for a long time now; sometimes they come and grab your purse and they insult you and throw things. The cops, they never come when you call.

□ I called them when these boys throwed rocks through my window. That policeman, he say, "What do you expect me to do about it?"

□ They don't care, you know they don't, long as no one gets killed, they don't even interfere in fights. They just drives by like they don't see nothin'.

Moreover, these police have a "bad attitude" toward the

tenants. In the tenants' terms, this means "looking down on" them, verbally abusing them and in general making their distaste for the tenants obvious. This "bad attitude," the tenants feel, merely reflects the attitude of the city and the Housing Authority.

The inspector in charge of the Hunters Point police, the liaison to the Potrero Hill Station, admits that the Housing Authority police rarely request help from the Potrero Hill Station except in cases of extreme emergencies such as murder (which he claims is no more frequent here than in the rest of the city, although there is a real reluctance on the part of the Housing Authority police to discuss crime rates in Hunters Point). The inspector says it is a quiet place with nice folks and "just like any other middle-class area of the city."

After delivering himself of these opinions he went on to reminisce about the good old days when there was a lot more fighting in the city.

Everybody used to fight a lot then; there was a lot of fight clubs. Everybody knew how to box and you could have some real good fights on Saturday night. We didn't care as much about fighting then as we do now, people I guess get more nervous about simple little fights than we used to. It used to lots of fun. People shouldn't get so upset by a little fighting nowadays, but I guess things have changed a lot. It's the same with all this talk about Bay pollution. Heck, we used to swim right near the sewer outlets' if you'd see a big one coming [a piece of human excrement] you'd just yell and duck.

The inspector was, of course, suggesting that although the general opinion of Hunters Point is that it's a dangerous place with a great deal of fighting, it is no different from the fighting he remembers as a boy in the Irish Mission district. More importantly, his suggestion that there was no particular problem of any type in Hunters Point showed that he wanted to relieve the Hunters Point police, as well as the city police, of their responsibilities, but apparently also to reduce racist attitudes which he obviously felt originated in white beliefs about those "dangerous Negroes."

The patrolmen themselves have a somewhat different attitude.

I been here 12 years and I could tell you some hair-raising stories about these people. Some of 'em—not all mind you 'cause there's some good ones—but some of 'em are no better'n animals. Yeah, you could find a lot of trouble if you go looking for it, but I don't. No, sir, I don't go looking for trouble—let 'em knock their own heads together.

But both positions have the same result: a tendency to lessen police activity within Hunters Point.

What constitutes a crime in Hunters Point? The police do not regard the kind of boisterous behavior frequently complained about by tenants (noisy parties, gambling in halls and stairways and the like) as a police matter. They feel that "this is not an upper-class neighborhood," a judgment based on the common sense observation that behavior is different in this neighborhood than it is in some others, and that it would only harass the population unnecessarily (and make police work harder) to police it strictly. Sophisticated as this view may be, it implies to many residents a paternalistic and racist attitude. Some tenants are infuriated that more or less illegal disturbances are thought to be tolerable since the people in Hunters Point "don't know no better." Yet at the same time, many of the same people are just as infuriated by attempts to enforce middle-class morality because they are aware of the racial and cultural prejudices that underlie such attempts.

Another reason why police are less active in Hunters Point than in other areas is that they cannot apply the common "on the beat" technique of harassing "suspicious-looking" people and people who are known to have criminal records or to associate with criminals. Clothing and appearance indicate only too well the "suspiciousness" of most of the young people in Hunters Point, while the criterion of prior criminality is meaningless since a large percentage of them have some record and many others do not only because of police leniency or luck. Verbal aggression and insulting gestures are so common that there is no official response to these either, though naturally they intensify hostility between police and tenants. In other parts of town automatic suspicion falls on young, male and poor blacks who seem sullen and aggressive. In Hunters Point so many fit this description that no one stands out.

This leaves the police with only their spies, or their own memories, to determine who should be watched. But in a neighborhood where police spies are despised even more than in most, and where black solidarity is gradually growing, few reliable informants exist. The Housing Authority police are often also frustrated in their attempts to solve the crimes that do occur. The most common complaints that can be acted on are of thefts and personal assaults, with thefts being far more common. But since theft is so common, disposal apparently so easy and the culprits so unlikely to be caught, the police characteristically do not try; in many cases (according to the residents) they do not even respond to reports. Moreover, most police, whether Housing Authority or city, correctly perceive the police-tenant relationship as a racial one and dread a massive incident that might arise as a result of some chance encounter, which is exactly what occurred. To avoid such encounters they involve themselves in the community as police only when no other alternative seems possible.

All these factors have resulted in observable under-policing in Hunters Point. But as a result of this very inactivity, police behavior may on occasion swing to the other extreme. Frustration and recognition of their own reduced importance may lead to periodic outbursts of excessive police brutality. Only so often can police fail to catch teenage thieves who escape them on foot before they lose control.

But the Hunters Point residents' response to under-policing is still a key factor in the climate that preceded the riot. They assume, often correctly, that police think of them merely as "animals" and don't care what they do to each other as long as they stay "on the Hill." They also feel that police do not become involved because they are afraid of the power and manliness of the Hunters Point males. This is an attractive view because it corresponds with the "super-spade" image, and it is partly correct in that many policemen do have such a fear. Indeed, in Hunters Point both groups are partly accurate in interpreting the attitudes of each other. This leads not to greater tolerance but to more and more unbearable tensions, which seem to need periodic release in outbursts of aggression on both sides.

The infamous Watts riots came before the Hunters Point riot, and Hunters Point residents commented at length on the Los Angeles situation. It was seen as a powerful expression of Negro strength, though in fact nearly all the victims of the riot were Negro. "We really showed them gray bastards" seems incongruous in the face of the fact that very little violence was directed against "grays" (Caucasions), with the exception of absent shopowners. Negro rioters in Watts did not leave Watts to attack whites. They simply did what Negroes have traditionally done and turned the violence as much on themselves as on others. This is an even clearer pattern in San Fransisco.

The police, however, aware of the hostility towards

them, are concerned about symbolic as well as real aggression. If it is true that frustration and prejudice combine to create explosive acts by police, they are able to do so even more among Negro males, and not all such aggressiveness is symbolic. While "being a man" is extremely important to the young Negro male, and his friends confirm him continuously as a "man," the police have a tendency not to treat him at all like a man. He is called "punk," "nigger bastard" and a variety of other obscene and degrading expressions. These threats hit too close to home for many teen-age Negro males. Many arrests and charges of "resisting arrest" or "assaulting an officer" originate from unbearable tongue-lashings by police which humiliate and emasculate young Negro males.

Police-resident relationships, then, are predictably unpredictable and unsatisfactory. The residents see police action as racially oppresive and police inaction as stemming from indifference or fear. These views are correct enough to receive support from each new confrontation. In this situation the police cannot be expected to enforce general social sanctions so that the community accepts them.

Public opinion as an alternative form of social control in Hunters Point is as ineffectual as the police. It mainly affects those younger than teen-age and over 50. Teen-agers, older teen-agers and people in their twenties—that is, those most likely to be involved in gambling, heavy drinking, fighting and theft—are least likely to be affected. This is true for several reasons. First, Hunters Point is not truly a community in the sense that its residents consciously try to identify with their neighbors. It is merely a place to live—or more accurately to sleep. Especially for young men and women, since they spend little time there, it does not represent "home" in any secure sense. Young men and women spend as much time as possible on Third Street at the foot of the Hill in the record shops, hamburger stands, bars and other amusement places that fill the street. Many try to spend most of their time in the Fillmore (another predominantly Negro district in San Francisco) or downtown. In Hunters Point itself there is nothing to do. Outside of playgrounds for children there are no organized amusement centers on the Hill.

Young males especially can afford to ignore the complaints of middle-aged women, since it is one of the few ways in which they can exhibit independence and superiority over females. Older blacks in general rightly see in the behavior of the young a reversal of the American Protestant tradition to which they themselves belong. While there was by the summer of 1967 little of the distinctive visual characteristics of black self-awareness, such as the "natural" hair style, the new standards were those of cool detachment, involving occasional drug use on the one hand, and rowdy male exhibitionism on the other.

The final major sanctioning agency in Hunters Point is the Housing Authority, but its main power, that of simply removing tenants (sometimes arbitrarily), is rapidly being reduced. In the absence of any other effective form of social control, then, what sanctions exist have come to correspond to the standards of the young, who are increasingly aware of the conflict between black and white, and are the more inclined to believe that what hurts a white man is justifiable on that account alone.

The police report of the incident is in the form of a very well organized pamphlet entitled *128 Hours*, the total length of the disturbance. This pamphlet details from the official police point of view the chronology of events during the disturbance. The report implies that the situation was handled by the San Fransisco police in an orderly and dignified fashion and that at no time was the situation inadequately understood by the police, who exhibited a general aura of competence. This report is at variance with some of the descriptions by individual police officers (none of whom can be named at this time for fear of prejudicing their positions) and is also at variance with the implications of the public press and the reportage of individuals who were present and/or arrested. Clearly these were not necessarily objective. Yet the police have an obvious vested interest as well. It is certain, however, that the police action did *not* result in any deaths after that of Matthew Johnson.

Johnson was shot on Tuesday, September 27, in a lot off Navy road, which runs through Hunters Point. A large crowd of people immediately gathered there. This crowd broke up in about two hours (4:00 p.m.). But, fearing Watts-style violence, the police tried to use so-called community leaders (black members of the city's Human Rights Commission) and confronted them with 70 or so black youths at a meeting in the Economic Opportunity Center on Third Street, just outside the Hunters Point housing site itself. Predictably, the Negro middle-class "community leaders" had absolutely no impact on the local men except to incense them further. The latter cared only that Officer Johnson be punished for "murder." This was understandable, but apparently not to the police.

The young men, consciously aware of their own economic deprivation, unconsciously responding to their precarious self-image and emboldened by the action of Negroes in Watts, were making every attempt to assert themselves in the face of this traditionally feared element of the white community (the police). They had also learned to despise successful middle-class Negroes as "Uncle Toms." Success in the white world is de facto evidence of "Tomming" to these young men.

The police now turned to the head of Youth for Service, supposedly an organization of ex-gang youths who operated as a liaison between the police and the fighting gangs.

This too, of course, was doomed to failure as the police had been misled by their belief that the Youth for Service leader controlled anything at all; gangs no longer existed in Hunters Point as a focus of any fighting activity or organizational strength.

A third tactical error was made in bringing Mayor John Shelley of San Francisco to address the crowd at Third Street near the Bayview Community Center. He indicated that Officer Johnson had been suspended pending an investigation of the incident. But the individuals who by this time were thinking in terms of "making their own little Watts" cared very little for the appearance of the mayor, who showed that he felt this one incident was central to the riot and that he was incapable of understanding the basic roots of discontent and its meaning in Hunters Point. Additionally, Mayor Shelley and other civic leaders, standing on the dignity of their offices, could not understand that their refusal to be "moved by violence" was interpreted as indifference and hate by the residents. As one of the rioters said some days later,

Shit man, that the first time the white motherfucker ever come down here to Hunters Point. Fuck man, we should riot every week, that get something out of that motherfucker.

In fact, the desire to move "the man" by violence, which would also negate personal feelings of inadequacy, was a core element of the situation.

Even more tragically, the Negro middle-class leadership failed to see that their presence could do no good and that they were not leaders of Hunters Point at all. They did not understand what the dispute was about, and they had no power to change the social situation. They expressed the view: "If they only realized what is being done for them and what we're all trying to do, they wouldn't riot." It was apparent that the "leaders" did not see that the "what was being done for them" was itself part of the package of frustrations leading to the disturbance.

The most eminent "Negro political leader" in the city, and the only one on the Board of Supervisors of the city, a man with a past record of leadership in the NAACP and as a defense lawyer in civil rights cases in the city, went with the mayor to Hunters Point to address the rioters and to try to calm them. If anything, he was greeted with greater antagonism than the mayor.

Rocks were thrown at the entourage, some of them narrowly missing both the mayor and the Negro supervisor, and the latter was completely unable to make himself heard. As one Hunters Pointer later put it,

That cocksucker forget he's black, but when we put them fuckers on the run, they sure let him know at City Hall right away. Sheeit, man, who the fuck he think he's foolin?

The Hunters Pointers felt that they saw the situation more realistically than the supervisor who was "fooling" himself into believing that he was actually accepted as an equal.

After a night of sporadic rioting, the "community leaders" (self-selected as well as those selected by the police and mayor) were unable to handle the situation. The police gave them a time limit on Wednesday afternoon. If at the end of an hour and a half they were still unable to control the situation, there would be police action in force to do so. These community leaders, many of whom were part of the matriarchal structure, as well as ministerial and poverty workers who were not part of it, were completely unable to control the situation. *There was nothing that they were empowered to offer the rioters in return for their stopping the riot which was even half as great as the reward for rioting itself.* Vague promises could not compensate for abandoning the sense of power which the riot gave its participants.

The police now called on the National Guard and other units of the Highway Patrol. At about 5:44 p.m. there was an incident which insured that the riot would not be brought under control quickly. Interestingly, the police report notes this incident in passing in the narrative section, and in the official police log of activities it is not noted at all, although it is the one incident all police officers involved in the riot and all Hunters Point residents recall. Police, in response, as they alleged, to gunfire being directed toward them from the Bayview Community Center, began to open fire on it. After riddling this frame building with every caliber of gun available, the police entered only to find several cowed and huddled children of pre-teen age and no evidence of any shooting or weapons in the building. The police did not kill any of the rioters, but the community now felt they wanted to and that they could expect no mercy. In fact, as well as overtly expressed anti-black attitudes, the police did engage in at least some willful property damage. Numerous bullet holes on a building 100 feet away from the community center indicate that it was gratuitously used as a target by police marksmen. Officers' reports confirm that some of their colleagues competed to see who could hit the gutterspout on top of the building. According to the reports, "Have you got your nigger today?" was a typical question, even though there seems to have been rather little shooting at people per se.

But not only was there some intentional shooting at unnecessary objects because of sport, some shooting occurred as a result of panic which struck the police officers (according to reports from individual police officers themselves). Just prior to the shooting, an officer was hit by a rock on his forehead. A small cut was opened, and the rumor was quickly passed, "They got one of our guys," and an unnamed sergant gave the order to fire at the Bayview Community Center. Many officers did so in panic.

This panic shows the extent to which white people in San Francisco have stereotyped notions of a Negro threat that far exceeds the evidence. These notions, which result in part from the projection of hatred onto Negroes and guilt over mistreatment of Negroes, have continued in full force even among police, who should actually be the more aware of the fact that Negro aggressiveness is almost always directed against other Negroes.

But by now the police were in no position to make discriminations between "good" Negroes and "bad" Negroes. Some Negro police officers, especially those in plain clothes, even after being identified, were mistreated and manhandled as well as attacked with derogatory racial epithets, as were (from their own reports) any number of otherwise inoffensive Negro middle-class types whose sin lay in the fact that they were the wrong color at the wrong time (one Negro informant was arrested and subsequently dismissed from his job although he was never convicted).

The Police Community Relations Unit, the very arm of the police force which was supposed to deal with minority groups, and whose head (since resigned) has an excellent reputation even among some of the most incorrigible criminals in the Hunters Point area, was not called into the area. Apart from the officer permanently attached to the area from the Community Relations Unit, no officer from this unit was assigned, according to members of the unit. Some officers on the force, both in and out of the unit, believe that this is because of racism in the department, or more mildly, a distrust of "soft tactics" when dealing with rioters.

However, the police undoubtedly considered the residents as riotous and dangerous long before they had become so, and this perception determined the actions of the police and finally the actions of the rioters. The police tend unconsciously to reinforce a Negro's fantasy image of himself as aggressive or dangerous in everyday encounters. In a riot, this will happen faster and more intensely. Moreover, in a riot there are no easy techniques of identification of friend or foe for the police to use except skin color, which becomes the sole criterion. Black skin equals rioter, white skin equals friend, so that there is even less chance to form a more sophisticated perception.

The next four days saw the riot continue with a decreasing incidence of violence and then finally peter out. A few fires were set, some windows broken; there was some looting along Third Street, but primarily the riot consisted of large numbers of "uncontrolled" Negroes moving along the streets. The damage, compared with riots in comparably sized cities, was minimal (several hundred thousand dollars), as were the casualties (ten civilians reported as victims of gunshot wounds with no serious casualties for the police or other antiriot personnel).

Perhaps the best indication of how passive the Negro response was in Hunters Point and how unreasonable the massive fears of whites is that there were less than half a dozen assults recorded by Negroes against whites in the course of five days of rioting. Far more violent acts than throwing bricks from a distance at police officers, breaking store windows and sporadic looting are possible in a large metropolitan area with a significant Negro population. There must have been some restraining factor other than the police at work. We suggest it was the internalized fear of whites, so difficult to break down, coupled with a "holiday mood." The riots were as much attempts to strengthen self-image as direct expressions of hatred and dissatisfaction with whites.

The police reaction is an interesting one. Until the beginning of the sixties, the police had dealt with Negro youths from Hunters Point by isolating them in Hunters Point. As one officer described his customary way of dealing with Negroes out of bounds, "Get back up on the Hill where you belong nigger. If I see your black ass down here again, I'll shoot it off." At the outbreak of the riots, though they were more or less city-wide, the same tactic was used. Negroes, no matter who they were or why they were in the Third Street area, were either arrested or pushed physically back up the Hill.

Even "moderate responsible" Negro adults feared that Negroes were being herded into Hunters Point so that they could be bombarded by naval vessels in the Bay. The fear was increased when an aircraft carrier in the Bay was seen passing Hunters Point. Panic, fear and a sense of total isolation from the United States as a social system typified the feelings of many residents.

When I was a boy in the army, I mean, man they was bringing in 90 millimeter recoilless rifles against us. I was scared. Man, that was what we was trained to use against the enemy. And that's what I was now—the enemy. I was just waiting for that carrier to send over planes and bomb us like they do in Vietnam.

However, there was some positive response as well. By Thursday the police report notes that youth peace patrols had been formed by some of the young men in Hunters Point, among them the few truly effective community leaders, who were aided as best they could be by the severely hampered Police Community Relations Unit supposedly attached to the Hunters Point area.

In spite of official approval for this group, many police officers saw those of their colleagues who supported it as "coddlers" who were trying to legitimize illegitimate Negro youth organizations (lumping together in their minds the nonexistent "bopping gangs," the poverty workers and other political activists). If blacks were automatically enemies, then to allow groups of them to do what the police could not do was bound to antagonize the more prejudiced members of the force.

Immediately after the riot, many residents of Hunters Point clearly hoped that the incidents of that fall would lead to greater solidarity among the different community groups and that many of the young men who had distinguished themselves in peace-making activities would gain prestige and power in the community.

Not only did this not happen, the opposite occurred. Even greater community disintegration resulted. The general belief that "nobody cares" and "it's too late to do anything" became widespread. Because they used military weapons and troops, the authorities were perceived by the residents as making full-scale war. Even "Uncle Toms," notorious for their prowhite attitude, have openly begun to state that they see whites as racists. Some residents have consequently formulated grandiose plans of "war" against white society or purchased small arms "to take some of them with us." Others who see these plans as deluded have simply given up hope and withdrawn.

The blatant and exclusive use by the police of the color criterion to decide whether or not to "rough you up" makes it very difficult for Negroes to continue communicating with whites in Hunters Point. Very few community organizations are still functioning. Even the long-existing Bayview Community Center now counts many pessimistic and cynical "time-servers" among its staff, and there is general feeling that it will soon close.

Very few people in Hunters Point now discuss the riots. Teenagers and young adult males now believe more strongly that they are seen as truly dangerous. This desperately wanted recognition has failed to remedy the causes of the feelings of inadequacy for which it compensates.

The white community has a fiction of its own for coping with this problem. Immediately after the riots, a consortium of local business leaders offered 2,000 jobs for

Hunters Point youths, to try to alleviate the severe unemployment problem. The jobs were to be channeled through the Youth Opportunity Center. These promises of steady fulltime or part-time work were made in October of 1966. By June 1967, 19 of these jobs had actually materialized.

As one of the staff at the Youth Opportunity Center indicated,

It is no longer possible to get the kids here to be enthusiastic about going for jobs—or waiting for all those jobs to come through. They just don't believe it will happen. They are right! After the first big rush of kids coming here for jobs after the riots, when no jobs happened, they just stopped coming. It's just as well; we don't have anything for them.

Probably the clearest aspect of the riot is that both black and white were and still are unable to see how deep are the disorders underlying this almost impotent attempt at self-assertion. Seriously in doubt of their own worth, and anyway denied the means of expressing it, young Negro men (and some women) in Hunters Point, without plan or forethought, drifted into an inept and inadequate revolt. At the same time, frightened beyond reason, perhaps through guilt, and certainly through their own paranoid projections and inadequate understanding of Hunters Point residents, the whites (police) underreacted, reacted wrongly, and finally overreacted to this confrontation.

Yet, there is something about the Hunters Point riots and white reaction to them that suggests that the United States had already institutionalized some method of handling these perceptions and misperceptions in symbolic form. Whites, on the whole, feel city-burnings to be too expensive to tolerate; Negroes generally seem to feel the danger of police reaction to be too dangerous to tolerate. Thus, both groups have compromised upon the "black militant aggressor" scenario as a substitute. In this scenario, young powerless Negroes are permitted the secondary rewards that riots give them. Permitted and indeed encouraged by whites to mouth revolutionary shibboleths, they are also allowed the *form* but not the *substance* of real manhood, independent thought and revolutionary political action. Meanwhile, more quiescent Negroes are given the opportunity of either decrying this "violence" and supporting their own passive role or of saying "I told you so" and thus at a distance identifying with the militants and safely, though vicariously, "bugging whites."

Sympathetic whites are permitted the luxury of indulging bravado militants while avoiding any dramatic structural changes that would give substance to the form of black power. Unsympathetic whites are permitted anger, fear and their own traditional paranoid concerns over "dangerous Negroes" and can view with alarm this formal rather than substantive militance.

Thus, the American game of black and white is played out. The perceptions and misperceptions of both races tend to stabilize race separation. Leakage out of this system is available only to a few "white" Negroes. Whites will fully integrate only nondangerous non-Negro Negroes.

A clear illustration of this is the increasingly prevalent belief among both black and white leaders that "separation" must precede "real integration." Black power separatism in this context is a "good thing," since only in "separation" can the black self-image improve. In fact, of course, Negroes and whites have *always* been separated in the United States. This "new" notion is surely no more than an attempt to formalize in the North what has always been true in the South. Until large numbers of Negroes began to live in the North, northerners could avoid dealing with their own racist feelings. Now, rather than face this racism openly and attempt to understand the cultural differences and psychological attitudes upon which this racism is based, whites are retreating from the problem by fostering separatism.

This, of course, fits the unconscious needs of some Negroes. Unable to "get into the game," except as white Negroes, many have taken on an outspoken "dangerous Negro" image. This helps overcome those feelings of inadequacy we have discussed. In this way, in an era of what appears to be very dynamic change in race relations in the United States, the status quo is actually maintained.

Hunters Point was early in the series of summer riots in the United States. The ones which followed became fiercer, partly because black youths felt that they had to do something "real bad to whitey" in order to feel more powerful, and partly because the white response came increasingly to be based on the "law and order" myth. If this chain reaction were to continue, then social catastrophe would certainly result. It would become plausible to predict full race war and concentration camps. But at any rate, the expected explosion in the cities in the summer of 1969 did not occur; and while militant blacks will no doubt develop more sophisticated techniques of action, it is likely that in the foreseeable future such action will remain symbolic. But if whites sustain their misperceptions and react without being aware of *what* black actions symbolize, then Americans can expect the worst.

San Francisco:
A Photographic Portfolio

MICHAEL ALEXANDER

Businessman, Haight-Ashbury

Upper Grant Avenue

Columbus Day

Mayor Joseph Alioto and gift

Financial district

File clerk, welfare department

Dead duck, Golden Gate Park

Sheraton-Palace Hotel

Sunday, Haight-Ashbury

North Beach bar

"Summer of Love," Haight-Ashbury

Sidewalk savior

Broadway

Friends, Union Square

Tenderloin district

Tourist and wife, Haight-Ashbury

Tourist and acquaintances, Broadway

Shoppers, Union Square

Boy with doll

Downtown

Tourist, "Summer of Love"

Saturday night

Parade, Golden Gate Park

Playground, Sunset district

Trudy on Telegraph Hill

Political rally, Civic Center

Marina Green

Golden Gate Park

Golden Gate Park

Near home, Union Street

From Sausalito

Friends and lovers, Union Street

The Health of Haight-Ashbury

DAVID E. SMITH/JOHN LUCE
ERNEST A. DERNBURG

Conventional middle-class populations receive the best care
our present conventional medical institutions can supply.
Middle-class people pay their bills on time or have health
insurance, which does it for them. They trust the doctor
to do what is best for them. They have diseases that go with
respectability, and the doctor who treats them need not
feel tainted by associating with people whose medical
problems arise from activities that are illegal or immoral.

People who do not measure up to middle-class standards
pose a problem for organized medicine. They require medical care no less than others, but the profession does not do
well in providing it. People who have no money or insurance, who mistrust doctors, who seem to the physician to
be immoral criminals, find it difficult to get care. Doctors
don't like them; they don't like the doctors. The profession, used to providing medical care in a style that suits it
and supplied with plenty of middle-class patients who
like that style, has never bothered to figure out how to de-

liver medical care in a way that suits other populations who live differently.

San Francisco's hippie invasion of 1967 created an acute problem of this kind. The city's officialdom made no adequate response to the medical and public health problems it produced, but a number of volunteers founded the Haight-Ashbury Free Medical Clinic, a unique experiment in providing medical care to a deviant population on terms it would accept. The story of the clinic—the problems of staffing, supplies, finances and the changing population needs it encountered—suggests some of the difficulties and some of the possibilities involved in such an innovation.

Three years ago *Time* magazine called San Francisco's Haight-Ashbury "the vibrant epicenter of America's hippie movement." Today the Haight-Ashbury District looks like a disaster area. Some of the wood frame Victorian houses, flats and apartment buildings lying between the Panhandle of Golden Gate Park and the northern slope of Mount Sutro have deteriorated beyond repair, and many property-owners have boarded over their windows or blocked their doorways with heavy iron bars. Hiding in their self-imposed internment, the original residents of the area seem emotionally exhausted and too terrified to leave their homes. "We're all frightened," says one 60-year-old member of the Haight-Ashbury Neighborhood Council. "The Haight has become a drug ghetto, a teen-age slum. The streets aren't safe; rats romp in the Panhandle; the neighborhood gets more run down every day. The only thing that'll save this place now is a massive dose of federal aid."

Nowhere is the aid more needed than on Haight Street, the strip of stores that runs east to west through the Flatlands. Once a prosperous shopping area, Haight Street has so degenerated by this time that the storefronts are covered with steel grates and sheets of plywood, while the sidewalks are littered with dog droppings, cigarette butts, garbage and broken glass. According to the owner of a small realty agency on the corner of Haight and Stanyan streets, over 50 grocers, florists, druggists, haberdashers and other merchants have moved off the street since the 1967 Summer of Love; property values have fallen 20 percent in the same period, but none of the remaining businessmen can find buyers for their stores. The Safeway Supermarket at Haight and Schrader streets has closed after being shoplifted out of $10,000 worth of merchandise in three months. The one shopowner to open since stocks padlocks and shatterproof window glass. "The only people making money on Haight Street now sell dope or cheap wine," the realtor claims. "Our former customers are all gone. There's nothing left of the old community anymore."

Nothing is left of the Haight-Ashbury's new hippie community today either. There are no paisley-painted buses on Haight Street, no "flower children" parading the sidewalks, no tribal gatherings, no H.I.P. (Haight Independent Proprietor) stores. Almost all the long-haired proprietors have followed the original merchants out of the district; the Psychedelic Shop at Haight and Clayton stands vacant; the Print Mint across the street and the Straight Theatre down the block are both closed. Allen Ginsberg, Timothy Leary, Ken Kesey and their contemporaries no longer visit the communal mecca they helped establish here in the mid-1960s. Nor do the rock musicians, poster artists and spiritual gurus who brought it international fame. And although a few young people calling themselves Diggers still operate a free bakery and housing office out of the basement of All Saints' Episcopal Church on Waller Street, Father Leon Harris there considers them a small and insignificant minority. "For all intents and purposes," he says, "the peaceful hippies we once knew have disappeared."

They started disappearing almost three years ago, when worldwide publicity brought a different and more disturbed

population to the Haight and the city escalated its unde-
clared war on the new community. Today, most of the
long-haired adolescents the public considers hip have left
Haight Street to hang out on Telegraph Avenue in Berkeley or on Grant Avenue in San Francisco's North Beach
District. Some of the "summer" hippies who once played
in the Haight-Ashbury have either returned home or reen-
rolled in school. Others have moved to the Mission District and other parts of the city, to Sausalito and Mill Valley
in Marin County, or Berkeley and Big Sur or to the rural
communes operating throughout northern California.

A few are still trapped in the Haight, but they take mescaline, LSD and other hallucinogenic drugs indoors and
stay as far away from Haight Street as possible. When
they must go there, to cash welfare checks or to shop at the
one remaining supermarket, they never go at night or walk
alone. "It's too dangerous for me," says one 19-year-old
unwed mother who ran away from a middle-class home in
Detroit during the summer of 1967. "Haight Street used
to be so groovy I could get high just being there. But I
don't know anybody on the street today. Since I've been
here, it's become the roughest part of town."

Responsible for the roughness is a new population that
has moved into the district and taken over Haight Street
like an occupying army. Transient and diverse, its members
now number several thousand persons. Included are a few
tourists, weekend visitors and young runaways who still
regard the Haight-Ashbury as a refuge for the alienated.
There are also older white, Negro and Indian alcoholics
from the city's Skid Row; black delinquents who live in the
Flatlands or the Fillmore ghetto; and Hell's Angels and
other "bikers" who roar through the area on their Harley
Davidsons. Finally there are the overtly psychotic young
people who abuse any and all kinds of drugs, and psycho-
pathic white adolescents with criminal records in San Fran-

cisco and other cities who come from lower-class homes or no homes at all.

Uneducated and lacking any mystical or spiritual interest, many of these young people have traveled from across the country to find money, stimulation and easy sex in the Haight and to exploit the flower children they assume are still living here. Some have grown long hair and assimilated the hip jargon in the process, but they resemble true hippies in no real way. "Street wise" and relatively aggressive in spite of the passive longings which prompt their drug abuse, they have little love for one another and no respect for the law or for themselves. Instead of beads and bright costumes they wear leather jackets and coarse, heavy clothes. Instead of ornate buses they drive beat-up motorcycles and hot rods. Although they smoke marijuana incessantly and drop acid on occasion, they generally dismiss these chemicals as child's play and prefer to intoxicate themselves with opiates, barbiturates and amphetamines.

Their individual tastes may vary, but most of the adolescents share a dreary, drug-based life-style. Few have any legal means of support, and since many are addicted to heroin, they must peddle chemicals, steal groceries and hustle spare change to stay alive. Even this is difficult, for there is very little money on Haight Street and a great deal of fear. Indeed, the possibility of being "burned," raped or "ripped off" is so omnipresent that most of the young people stay by themselves and try to numb their anxiety and depression under a toxic fog. By day they sit and slouch separately against the boarded-up storefronts in a drug-induced somnolence. At night they lock themselves indoors, inject heroin and plan what houses in the district they will subsequently rob.

Although the results of this living pattern are amply reflected in the statistics available from Park Police Station at Stanyan and Waller streets, the 106 patrolmen there are apparently unable to curb the Haight-Ashbury's crime. Their job has been made easier by the relative decrease in amphetamine consumption and the disappearance of many speed freaks from the district over the past few months, but the rate of robbery and other acts associated with heroin continues to rise. Making regular sweeps of Haight Street in patrol cars and paddy wagons, the police also threaten to plant drugs on known dealers if they will not voluntarily leave town. Yet these and other extreme measures seem only to act like a negative filter in the Haight, screening out the more cunning abusers and leaving their desperate counterparts behind.

Futhermore, the narcotics agents responsible for the Haight-Ashbury cannot begin to regulate its drug flow. According to one agent of the State Narcotics Bureau, "The Haight is still the national spawning ground for multiple drug abuse. The adolescents there have caused one of the toughest law enforcement problems we've ever known."

They have also created one of the most serious health problems in all of San Francisco. Many of the young people who hang out on Haight Street are not only overtly or potentially psychotic, but also physically ravaged by one another as well. Although murder is not particularly popular with the new population, some of its members seem to spend their lives in plaster casts. Others frequently exhibit suppurating abrasions, knife and razor slashes, damaged genitalia and other types of traumatic injuries—injuries all caused by violence.

Even more visible is the violence they do to themselves. Continually stoned on drugs, the adolescents often over-exert and fail to notice as they infect and mangle their feet by wading through the droppings and broken glass. Futhermore, although some of the heroin addicts lead a comparatively stabilized existence, others overlook the physical deterioration which results from their self-destructive life-styles. The eating habits of these young people are so poor that they are often malnourished and inordinately susceptible to infectious disease. In fact, a few of them suffer from protein and vitamin deficiencies that are usually found only in chronic alcoholics three times their age.

With gums bleeding from pyorrhea and rotting teeth, some also have abscesses and a diffuse tissue infection called cellulitis, both caused by using dirty needles. Others miss their veins while shooting up or rupture them by injecting impure and undissolvable chemicals. And since most sleep, take drugs and have sex in unsanitary environments, they constantly expose themselves to upper respiratory tract infections, skin rashes, bronchitis, tonsillitis, influenza, dysentery, urinary and genital tract infections, hepatitis and venereal disease.

In addition to these and other chronic illnesses, the young people also suffer from a wide range of drug problems. Some have acute difficulties, such as those individuals who oversedate themselves with barbiturates or "overamp" with amphetamines. Others have chronic complaints, longterm "speed"-precipitated psychoses and paranoid, schizophrenic reactions. Many require physical and psychological withdrawal from barbiturates and heroin. In fact, heroin addiction and its attendant symptoms have reached epidemic proportions in the Haight-Ashbury, and the few doctors at Park Emergency Hospital cannot check the spread of disease and drug abuse through the district any better than the police can control its crime.

To make matters worse, these physicians appear unwilling to attempt to solve the local health problems. Like many policemen, the public health representatives seem to look on young drug abusers as subhuman. When adolescents come to Park Emergency for help the doctors frequently assault them with sermons, report them to the police or submit them to complicated and drawn-out referral procedures that only intensify their agony. The nurses sometimes tell prospective patients to take their problems elsewhere. The ambulance drivers simply "forget" calls for emergency assistance. They and the other staff members apparently believe that the best way to stamp out sickness in the Haight is to let its younger residents destroy themselves.

Given this attitude, it is hardly surprising that the adolescents are as frightened of public health officials as they are of policemen. Some would sooner risk death than seek aid at Park Emergency and are equally unwilling to go to San Francisco General Hospital, the city's central receiving unit, two miles away. Many merely live with their symptoms, doctor themselves with home remedies or narcotize themselves to relieve their pain. These young people do not trust "straight" private physicians, who they assume will overcharge them and hand them over to the law. Uneducated about medical matters, they too often listen only to the "witch doctors" and drug-dealers who prowl the Haight-Ashbury, prescribing their own products for practically every physical and psychological ill.

A few are receptive to responsible opinion and anxious to be properly treated, particularly those individuals who want to kick heroin and those younger adolescents who have just made the Haight their home. Unfortunately, however, they have nowhere to go for help. Huckleberry's for Runaways and almost all the other service agencies created to assist the hippies in 1967 have suspended operations in the area. Although Father Harris and several other neighborhood ministers offer free advice at their respective churches, they can hardly deal with all the young people who come their way. Indeed, the only major organization that can reach the new population is the Haight-Ashbury

Free Medical Clinic. But today, the first privately operated facility in America to employ community volunteers in providing free and nonpunitive treatment of adolescent drug and health difficulties has serious problems of its own.

This is ironic, for although it is still somewhat at odds with the local medical Establishment, the clinic is better staffed and funded than at any point is its 3-year history. It is also more decentralized, with several facilities in and outside of the Haight-Ashbury. Its oldest operation, a Medical Section located on the second floor of a faded yellow building at the corner of Haight and Clayton streets, is now open from six until ten five evenings a week. Over 40 dedicated volunteers are on hand in the 14-room former dentist's office, so that 558 Clayton Street can accommodate more than 50 patients a day.

Of the young people who use the facility, only half live in the immediate area. The rest are hippies, beats and older people who come with their children from as far away as southern California. Accepting the clinic because it accepts them, the patients are treated by a staff of over 20 volunteer nurses and physicians in an atmosphere brightened by poster art and psychedelic paraphernalia. Some of these health professionals are general practitioners committed to community medicine. Others are specialists hoping to broaden their medical understanding. Many are interns and residents looking for experience or studying the Medical Section as a philosophic alternative to the practices of the Public Health Department and the American Medical Association.

Whatever their motivation, the doctors' primary objectives are diagnosis and detoxification. After examining their patients, they attempt to treat some with donated drugs which are kept under lock and key in the clinic pharmacy. Others require blood, urine and vaginal smear tests that can be performed in the laboratory on equipment furnished by the Medical Logistics Company of San Francisco and its 35-year-old president, Donald Reddick, who serves as the clinic's administrative director. Most of the patients have chronic problems, however, and cannot be treated adequately on the premises. They must therefore be referred and/or physically transported to other facilities, such as Planned Parenthood, the Society for Humane Abortions, the Pediatrics Clinic at the University of California Medical Center on Parnassus Street six blocks south, Children's Hospital, San Francisco General Hospital and the Public Health Department Clinic for VD. The Medical Section maintains a close working relationship with these institutions and can therefore act as a buffer between its hip patients and the straight world.

Although the physicians and nurses contribute to this mediating process, much of the referring, chauffeuring and patient-contracting at 558 Clayton Street is carried out by its staff of clerks, administrative aides and paramedical volunteers. Twenty such young people donate their time and energy to the Medical Section at present, most of them student activists, conscientious objectors fulfilling alternative service requirements and former members of the Haight-Ashbury's new community. Emotionally equipped to handle the demands and the depressing climate of ghetto medicine, several core members of the paramedical staff live together in the Haight as a communal family.

Supervising the volunteers is Dr. Alan Matzger, a 37-year-old surgeon from San Francisco who developed an interest in community medicine after working at 558 Clayton Street for over a year. The clinic's first full-time resident physician, Dr. Matzger is actually employed by the United States Public Health Service, which has asked him to conduct a long-range investigation of health needs in the Haight-Ashbury. He is now nearing completion of this study and will soon develop an objective and comprehensive plan for community medical care.

Since heroin addiction is such a pressing current problem, Dr. Matzger and an anesthesiologist named Dr. George Gay have recently launched a heroin withdrawal program at the Medical Section. Working there five afternoons a week for the past four months, the two physicians have treated over 200 patients, less than 50 percent of whom consider the Haight their home. "The remainder are adolescents from so-called good families," Dr. Gay reports, "most of them students at local colleges and high schools. Significantly, they follow the same evolutionary pattern as young pople have in this district, progressing from hallucinogenic drug abuse to abuse of amphetamines and then to abuse of barbiturates and opiates. The 'Year of the Middle-Class Junkie' in San Francisco may well be 1970. If it is, we hope to expand our program as addiction problems mount throughout the entire Bay area."

Another expansion underway at the clinic is a dentistry service. Organized by Dr. Ira Handelsman, a dentist from the University of the Pacific who is paid by a Public Health Service grant to study periodontal disease, this is the first free program of dentistry in the city outside of the oral surgery unit at San Francisco General Hospital where teeth are extracted, not repaired. As such, the service is under fire from the local dental society, which is opposed to this form of free dental care. Nevertheless, Dr. Handelsman is committed to his effort and has recently secured three donated dental chairs.

Although this and other programs at 558 Clayton Street are intended to operate somewhat autonomously, they are closely coordinated with those operated out of the clinic's second center in the Haight-Ashbury. Known as "409 House," it is located in a pale blue Victorian residence at the corner of Clayton and Oak streets, across from the panhandle. On the first floor of this building is a reading and mediation room supervised by Reverend Lyle Grosjean of the Episcopal Peace Fellowship who counsels some adolescents about spiritual, marital, draft and welfare problems and offers shelter for others coming in from the cold.

On the third floor at 409 Clayton Street is the clinic publications office, staffed by volunteers who oversee the preparation of *The Journal of Psychedelic Drugs*, a semi-annual compilation of articles and papers presented at the drug symposia sponsored by the clinic and the University of California Medical Center Psychopharmacology Study Group. Aided by several health professionals, the volunteers also answer requests for medical information and administer the affairs of the National Free Clinics Council, an organization created in 1968 for the dozens of free facilities in Berkeley, Boston and other cities that modeled their efforts after those of the Haight-Ashbury Free Medical Clinic programs.

Sandwiched in between the Publications Office and Reverend Grosjean's sanctuary is the Psychiatric Section. This service, which is supervised by Stuart Loomis, a 47-year-old associate professor of education at San Francisco State College, provides free counseling and psychiatric aid for over 150 individuals. Roughly one-half of these patients are hippies and "active hippies" who either live in the district or commute from rural and urban communes where physicians from the Medical Section make house calls. The remaining 50 percent is made up of young people who suffer from the chronic anxiety and depression common in heroin addicts.

Loomis and the other 30 staff psychologists, psychiatrists and psychiatric social workers at 409 Clayton Street are able to counsel some of these patients in the Psychiatric Section. They usually refer the more disturbed multiple drug-abusers and ambulatory schizophrenics now common to the Haight either to such facilities as the drug program at Mendicino State Hospital or to the Immediate Psychiatric Aid and Referral Service at San Francisco General, whose director, Dr. Arthur Carfagni, is on the clinic's executive committee. When intensive psychiatric intervention is not called for, however, they frequently send the patients to the clinic's own Drug Treatment Program in the basement downstairs.

Although fed by beats and students from San Francisco State, this colony remained unnoticed for several years. One reason was its members' preference for sedating themselves with alcohol and marijuana instead of using drugs that attract more attention. Another was their preoccupation with art and their habit of living as couples or alone. This living pattern was drastically altered in 1964, however, with the popular acceptance of mescaline, LSD and other hallucinogens and the advent of the Ginsberg-Leary-Kesey nomadic, passive, communal electric and acid-oriented life-style. The beats were particularly vulnerable to psychoactive chemicals that they thought enhanced their aesthetic powers and alleviated their isolation. Because of this, hallucinogenic drugs swept the Haight-Ashbury, as rock groups began preparing in the Flatlands what would soon be known as the "San Francisco Sound." On January 1, 1966 the world's first Psychedelic Shop was opened on Haight Street. Two weeks later, Ken Kesey hosted a Trips Festival at Longshoreman's Hall. Fifteen thousand individuals attended, and the word "hippie" was born. A year later, after Diggers and HIP had come to the Haight, the new community held a tribal gathering for 20,000 white Indians on the polo fields of Golden Gate Park. At this first Human Be-In, it showed its collective strength to the world.

The community grew immeasurably in size and stature as a result of this venture, but the ensuing publicity brought

90/DAVID E. SMITH, JOHN LUCE & ERNEST A. DERNBURG

it problems for which its founders were ill prepared. In particular, the immigration of more young people to the Haight-Ashbury after the Be-In caused a shortage in sleeping space and precipitated the emergence of a new living unit, the crash pad. Adolescents forced to reside in these temporary and overcrowded structures started to experience adverse hallucinogenic drug reactions and psychological problems. The new community began to resemble a gypsy encampment, whose members were exposing themselves to an extreme amount of infectious disease.

Theoretically, the San Francisco Public Health Department should have responded positively to the situation. But instead of trying to educate and treat the hippies, it attempted to isolate and thereby destroy their community. Still convinced that theirs was a therapeutic alternative, the young people packed together in the Haight grew suicidally self-reliant, bought their medications on the black market and stocked cases of the antipsychotic agent Thorazine in their crash pads. Meanwhile, the Diggers announced that 100,000 adolescents dropping acid in Des Moines and Sioux Falls would flock to the Haight-Ashbury when school was out. They then tried to blackmail the city into giving them the food, shelter and medical supplies necessary to care for the summer invasion.

Although the Public Health Department remained unmoved by the Diggers' forecast, a number of physicians and other persons associated with the University of California Psychopharmachology Study Group did react to the grisly promise of the Summer of Love. Among them were Robert Conrich, a former private investigator turned bohemian; Charles Fischer, a dental student; Dr. Frederick Meyers, internationally respected professor of pharmacology at the Medical Center; and Dr. David Smith, a toxicologist who was then serving as chief of the Alcohol and Drug Abuse Screening Unit at General Hospital. Several of these men lived in or were loyal to the Haight-Ashbury. Many had experience in treating bad LSD trips and felt that a rash of them would soon occur in the district. All had contacts among the new community and were impressed by the hippies' dreams of new social forms. But they also knew that the hippies did not number health among their primary concerns, although they might if they were afforded a free and accepting facility. In April then they decided to organize a volunteer-staffed crisis center which might answer the growing medical emergency in the area.

As they expected, the organizers had little difficulty in gathering a number of hip and straight persons for their staff. However, they did face several problems in implementing their plans. First, they were unable to find space in the Haight until Robert Conrich located an abandoned dentist's office and obtained a lease for one-half of its 14 rooms. Paying the rent then became problematical, but Stuart Loomis and an English professor from State College, Leonard Wolf, offered funds if they could use half the facility for an educational project called Happening House. Finally, the organizers learned that local zoning regulations prohibited the charity operation they envisioned. This obstacle was overcome only after a sympathetic city Supervisor, Jack Morrison, suggested that Dr. Smith establish the clinic as his private office so that his personal malpractice insurance could cover its volunteers.

Once this was accomplished, the organizers dredged up an odd assortment of medical equipment from the basements of several local hospitals. Utilizing the University of California Pharmacology Department, they also contacted the "detail men" representing most of America's large pharmaceutical houses and came up with a storeroom full of donated medications, including some vitally needed Thorazine. They then furnished a calm center for treating adverse LSD reactions at the facility.

Next, the organizers told the Public Health Department of their efforts. Its director, Dr. Ellis Sox, indicated that he might reimburse the organizers or open his own medical center if it was required in the Haight-Ashbury. Encouraged by this, the organizers alerted the new community that they would soon be in business. On the morning of June 7, 1967 the door to 558 Clayton Street was painted with the clinic's logo, a white dove of peace over a blue cross. Underneath this was written its slogan, Love Needs Care. The need itself was demonstrated that afternoon when the door was opened and 200 patients pushed their way inside.

Although the organizers anticipated the need for a regional health center in the Haight, they never dreamed that so many adolescents would seek help at the Medical Section. Nor did they suspect that the Diggers would be so close in their estimate of the number of individuals coming to the district that summer. Not all 100,000 showed up at once, but at least that many visitors did pass through the Haight-Ashbury during the next three months, over 20,000 of them stopping off at 558 Clayton Street along the way. A quarter of these persons were found to be beats, hippies and other early residents of the area. A half were "summer" hippies, comparatively healthy young people who experimented with drugs and might have done so at Fort Lauderdale and other locations had not the media told them to go West. The final quarter were bikers, psychotics and psychopaths of all ages who came to exploit the psychedelic scene.

Most of these individuals differed psychologically, but sickness and drugs were two things they all had in common. Some picked up measles, influenza, streptococcal pharyngitis, hepatitis, urinary and genital tract infections and venereal disease over the summer. Uncontrolled drug experimentation was rampant so others had bad trips from the black-market acid flooding the area. Many also suffered adverse reactions from other drugs, for the presence of psychopaths and multiple abusers brought changes in pyschoactive chemical consumption on the street. This first became obvious at the Summer Solstice Festival, where 5,000 tablets were distributed containing the psychomimetic amphetamine STP. Over 150 adolescents were treated for STP intoxication at the clinic, and after an educational program was launched, the substance waned in popularity in the district. But many of its younger residents had sampled intensive central nervous system stimulation for the first time during the STP episode. As a result, many were tempted to experiment next with "speed."

Such experimentation increased over the summer, until the Haight became the home of two separate subcultures, the first made up of "acid heads" who preferred hallucinogens, the second consisting of "speed freaks" partial to amphetamines. At the same time, the district saw the emergence of two different life-styles, the first characterized by milder adolescent illnesses, the second marked by malnutrition, cellulitis, tachycardia, overstimulation and the paranoid-schizophrenic reactions associated with "speed." This naturally affected the calm center, where student volunteers were treating more than 50 adverse drug reactions every 24 hours. It also made extreme demands on the doctors in the Medical Section, who were dealing with more than 250 patients a day. Discouraged and exhausted by their efforts, the physicians pleaded with the Public Health Department for assistance. Yet the department refused to help the facility and never attempted to open a crisis center of its own.

Fortunately, this refusal did not pass unnoticed by the

local press, and 558 Clayton Street received a great deal
of community aid. Shortly after the clinic's plight was
reported, the facility was flooded with doctors disappointed
by the Public Health Department and with medical
students who came from as far as Indiana to volunteer.
Several Neighborhood Council members dropped by with
food for the workers, while contributions began arriving
through the mail. One of us (Dernburg) and more than 30
other psychiatrists arrived at 558 Clayton Street and
established a temporary Psychiatric Section on the
premises. They were followed by Donald Reddick and his
partners in Medical Logistics, who donated over $20,000
worth of equipment and organized the staff procedures
along with more efficient lines. The second set of seven
rooms was leased; a laboratory, pharmacy and expanded
calm center were installed. Then Dr. William Nesbitt,
a general practitioner, invited the organizers to join Youth
Projects, an agency he headed, and to use its nonprofit
status to accept donations. When all was completed, the
clinic was the best-equipped neighborhood center in town.

It was also the most chaotic, of course, a fact that was
causing increased friction with the psychiatric staff, and
with Dr. Leonard Wolf, who had never been able to create
his Happening House because the Medical Section was so
crowded. Once the clinic annex at 409 Clayton Street
was furnished, however, Dr. Wolf was given space for his
classroom. A Psychiatric Section was also established, so
the doctors were able to counsel young people in relative
privacy, to segregate the more violent amphetamine-
abusers and to reduce the traffic in the Medical Section
to a more manageable flow.

While this was going on, the clinic was also involving
itself in the crumbling new community. *Time* and other
publications somehow assumed that the Haight was still
full of hippies at this point, but the physicians at 558

Clayton Street knew otherwise. Realizing that the district was becoming even more disorganized, they created an informal council with Huckleberry's for Runaways, All Saints', the Haight-Ashbury Switchboard and other groups trying to prevent its total collapse. They then launched *The Journal of Psychedelic Drugs* to disseminate pharmacological information and started to participate more actively in community town hall meetings at the Straight Theatre. These several activities greatly enhanced the clinic's reputation in and outside of the Haight-Ashbury.

Although this publicity proved helpful to the facility in certain respects, it also caused several new crises. The first occurred two days after the publication of a *Look* magazine article by John Luce on the clinic, when Dr. Smith was notified that his malpractice insurance was to be cancelled because he was "working with those weirdos in the Haight." This crisis was resolved when Dr. Robert Morris, a pathologist who was then chairman of the executive committee, suggested that he apply for group coverage under the auspices of the San Francisco Medical Society. Dr. Smith doubted that this organization would ever support his advocacy of free medical care. He was therefore delighted when the Medical Society not only granted him membership but also endorsed the programs at 558 and 409 Clayton Street.

His delight did not last long, however, for shortly after the endorsement the clinic had to contend with a number of persons who tried to capitalize on its good name. First were a number of bogus doctors, most of whom worked under stolen or forged medical licenses in the Haight-Ashbury. Then came the Diggers, who resented the facility's influence in the community. Finally, the Medical Section was besieged by several older psychopaths, one of whom hoped to turn it into his base of operations in the Haight. This person was ultimately exposed and run out of the clinic, but shortly after he left, Robert Conrich, who was close to collapse after serving for two months as administrator, retired.

Although a severe blow in itself, Conrich's departure was also an ill omen. In fact, less than a week after he tendered his resignation, the Medical Section ran out of funds. The volunteers rallied to meet this new crisis; phone calls were made to potential contributors; and several paramedical staff members begged for money on Haight Street. Two dance-concert benefits with local rock groups that used the facility were also held, but only one was successful. In desperation, Peter Shubart called Joan Baez, who helped take patient histories and sang to entertain the lonely youngsters as they sat quietly in the waiting room. Yet even she could not save the clinic. On September 22 the door was locked at 558 Clayton Street. Two weeks later, what was left of the new community held a "Death of Hip" ceremony to bury the term "hippie" and remove the media from its back. "Haight used to be love," a participant wrote on the steps of the Medical Section after the event. "Now, where has all the love gone?"

This question could be easily answered, for by the end of the Summer of Love almost all of the original hippies had moved to urban and rural communes outside of the Haight. Many summer hippies had also left the district, and those who remained either fended for themselves or were assimilated into the new population. Staying in the Haight-Ashbury, they quickly changed from experimental drug-users into multiple abusers and needed even more help. For this reason, the clinic organizers were determined to open the Medical Section again.

At the same time, they had another good reason to renew their efforts in the Haight. With the hippie movement spread across the United States by this point, other cities—

Seattle, Boston, Berkeley, Cambridge, even Honolulu—
were being swept by drug problems. New clinics were
being created in the face of this onslaught, all of them
looking to the Haight-Ashbury for guidance. Although
always a confused and crisis-oriented center, the Haight-
Ashbury Free Medical Clinic had become the national
symbol of a new and successful approach in reaching a
deviant popluation of alienated adolescents. Thus, its
organizers had not only their medical practice but also their
position of leadership to resume.

However, not all of them could still work in the Haight, a
few were turning to other projects; Peter Shubart resumed
his studies in biochemistry; and others went back to prior
commitments such as teaching.

But in spite of the losses the organizers looked to what
was left of the new community for support. Another dance-
concert benefit was held, this one under the guidance of
Fillmore Auditorium owner Bill Graham, and several
thousand dollars were raised. Smaller events were hosted
at the Straight Theatre and at the John Boles Gallery.
In addition, a wealthy local artist named Norman Stone
stepped forward to finance a substantial part of the Medical
Section program. The clinic had still received no private
or public grants, but by the end of October it had the funds
necessary to open again.

When operations were resumed, however, the staff had
a great deal more speed and more violence to contend with.
In late February of 1968 a tourist ran over a dog,
prompting a large crowd of adolescents to assemble on
Haight Street. This in turn allowed Mayor Joseph Alioto
to unleash his latest weapon for crime control, the 38-man
Tactical Squad. After cleaning the street with tear gas
and billies that afternoon, the squad vowed to return and
enforce its own type of law and order. It did so four months
later, when the district was ripped by three nights of

rioting, rock-throwing and fires.

After the flames died down, it became apparent that the disturbance had marked yet another turning point in the history of the clinic. Many of its nurses, doctors and para-medical volunteers interpreted the riot as a sign that the Haight was now hopeless; mail contributions also ceased; and several psychiatrists who felt they could do little with or for the new population resigned from their positions. Low on money at this point, the clinic's business manager decided to host a three-day fund-raising benefit over the Labor Day weekend at the Palace of Fine Arts. The Affair was sabotaged by Major Alioto, who denied the cooperation of his Park and Recreation Commission. When the benefit, Festival of Performing Arts, was finally over, the organizers had lost $20,000. Two days later, the Medical Section was once again closed.

The second clinic closing was followed by another exodus, as Dr. Dernburg, Dr. Morris, Dr. Meyers and others decided that their efforts were fruitless in the Haight. Fund-raising and new recruiting proved difficult, because the public was tired of the distrust.

But, in spite of these obstacles, some progress was made. First, one of us (Smith) was awarded a grant to study adverse marijuana reactions which could be run in conjunction with the clinic. Stuart Loomis was installed as chief of the Psychiatric Section; Roger Smith and John Frykman raised more money for the Drug Treatment Program. In December the clinic received financial pledges from Norman Stone, the San Francisco Foundation and the Mary Crocker Trust. By January 7, 1969, 558 Clayton Street was in business again.

In contrast to previous years, its business went relatively smoothly in 1969. The amphetamines gradually ran their course in the district, and many of the multiple drug-abusers here switched to opiates, barbiturates and other

"downers" after becoming too "strung out" on "speed."
This change in chemical consumption naturally affected
treatment practices, as heroin addiction increased tenfold
and young people suffered even more types of chronic
illness as a result of their drug abuse. Yet, in spite of the
new population's problems, the year was a productive one
for the clinic. Over 20,000 patients were treated at the
Medical and Psychiatric Sections; research programs were
initiated; efforts were made to reach the hippies in their
communes; the volunteers became more experienced,
although fewer in number; and Dr. Dernburg, Dr. Meyers
and other ex-staff members became involved in treatment
programs of their own.

This year has also been a period of growth. More grants
have been secured, and the inclusion of the Drug Treatment Program in the Northeast Mental Health Center,
which provides for 14 new paid staff positions, has meant
the facility's first official recognition by a public agency.
In sum, the Haight-Ashbury Free Medical Clinic has
finally become established—and, some say, part of the
Establishment. From its third opening until the present, it
has enjoyed a time of expansion, improvement and relative
peace.

Whether these conditions continue depends, as always,
on the Haight-Ashbury. This is particularly true today because its resident population seems to be changing once
again. As some of the drug-abusers drift out of the area,
their places are apparently being taken by adventurous college students. More black delinquents from the Fillmore
ghetto are also frequenting the district, contributing to its
heroin problem, though participating in the Drug Treatment Program for the first time. The Neighborhood Council and Merchants' Association still function, but both
are demoralized and at a political impasse. In addition, the
area is seeing an increased influx of older Negro families.

Because of this, some staff members are urging changes at Medical and Psychiatric Sections. One faction sees the clinic evolving into a health center for the entire neighborhood and wants to purchase one of the abandoned buildings on Haight Street so that all future programs can be consolidated under one roof. Another argues for more decentralization, de-emphasis of certain activities and/or increased expansion within and without the Haight.

Dr. Matzger, who knows the district intimately, has not yet decided what policy changes will stem from his United States Public Health Service study. However, he does not feel that both 409 and 558 Clayton Street will be different tomorrow from what they are today. "The clinic is at a crossroads," he says. "It may continue as a screening, diagnosis, detoxification and referral unit. It may become an expanded Drug Treatment Program. It may evolve into a large neighborhood health facility, particularly if we get the required dose of federal aid. On the other hand, it may have to cut back on some of the present programs. But whatever happens, it will continue to be an amalgam of individual efforts and an inspiration to people who seek new approaches in community medicine. Furthermore, no matter how the Haight-Ashbury changes, we hope that the clinic will never close again."

The Politics of Hyperpluralism

FREDERICK M. WIRT

Because, as Alexander Hamilton noted, men are not angels, government is needed; but from the beginning the makers of American charters have been almost obsessed by fears of too much government. The Platonic method of controlling arbitrary power—by recruiting only moral men—has found limited use in our history. It is Aristotle who informs the American political tradition: the division of power so that no one gets too much—power is set against power, ambition against ambition and interest against interest. The hope is that in this way, "Nobody gets everything, nobody gets nothing, everybody gets something."

Few American cities have embraced this traditional principle more enthusiastically than San Francisco. Here the politics of public decision-making proceeds in a context of such fragmentation of power that the traditional principle has come to its logical end—powerlessness. In this article, part of a larger work in progress, I treat but one question: How are political decisions made here? The answers tell us

101

much about the adaptability of this political structure to meet emergent community problems and to respond to group demands.

Political decisions are our focus, those having a public impact and those most often in the domain of government. Decisions that arise out of private organizations also have public consequences, of course, and hence they too are a part of the pool of political decisions. When the Transamerica Corporation decides to erect a gigantic skyscraper in downtown San Franciso, it will have immense effect on many city dwellers. Although I won't discuss this sort of decision here, one has to keep in mind that this world of private decision-makers exists and that it is made up of both a Big Establishment and a Small Establishment. The distinction is not merely the amounts of money available to each. The Big E is peopled by financial and industrial capitalists and managers whose interests run far beyond the Bay to the nation and the world. The Small E centers on the group whose financial interests extend only to the Bay Area, and particularly the city itself.

The Big E pays little attention to San Francisco politics or its government, while many in the Small E do so with perserverance and fascination. Both have material interests at stake in local government, of course, but the Big E's are long-run, while the Small E's are short-run. Both cooperate on cultural, civic and generally nonpolitical matters. And in the last analysis, one can safely suppose that it is this constellation of private interests that makes many if not most of the decisions that allocate values in this community and that therefore affect most people most enduringly. Government, however, often has to deal with many of the problems that arise as the result of these private decisions. Local government may have little to do with the origins of such problems; it may not help in the takeoff, but only in the flight—and often only when cries of "Mayday! Mayday!" fill the air.

For anyone accustomed to the frenetic party politics of such big American cities as Chicago, Detroit, New York and Boston, the party politics of California cities must seem mysterious, if only because of their absence. Like the dog in the Sherlock Holmes story, they are important because they do *not* bark. One finds traces of their presence in party leader titles and in announcements of committee meetings. But such spoor lead to nothing at all.

The evanescent nature of California parties arises from the state's distinctive political culture. Its central feature is a distrust of politics and politicians and a magical belief that if you give something a different name, you can change its essential quality—like the Victorians calling chicken breast "white meat." But the abolition of political parties didn't make politicians and politics vanish. They only shifted their field of operations into what Eugene C. Lee has described in *The Politics of Nonpartisanship* as a "politics of acquaintance" in which one's political loyalties and values are shaped by friends and neighbors, or by specific interests close to one's heart or pocketbook.

Such is the politics of the city of San Francisco today, although it was not always so. Before World War II, the Irish totally dominated Democratic politics; but in the post-World War II period their dominance began to loosen. Both parties now reveal a high degree of factionalism, and it is not uncommon to see interparty coalitions on behalf of specific candidates or issues.

Among the Democrats there had been hopes in the late 1950s that the California Democratic Council (CDC) would permanently consolidate and lead a liberal movement. The CDC now controls the party's Central Committee in the county (identical with the city as the two are consolidated). But the fervor generated by Adlai Stevenson has diffused lately, so much so that in the 1968 presidential primary, Democrats provided Humphrey, Kennedy and McCarthy with slates of delegates.

This fragmentation is well illustrated in the 1967 election of the dominant political figure of San Francisco today, Mayor Joseph Alioto. First of all, the basic rule of the game in such races is that victory is by plurality—highest takes all. This plurality system clearly militates against coalitions, which would be needed if a runoff election were required to achieve a majority winner. Fragmentation is thereby enhanced. Thus in the 1967 contest there were three candidates: Alioto; Jack Morrison, Democratic member of the Board of Supervisors (the legislative body under city-county consolidation); and Harold Dobbs, the Republican. All of this, remember, was formally nonpartisan.

Alioto's victory that fall was deliberately built on the support of a number of factions. When the rising Democratic leader, State Senator Eugene McAteer, died in the spring of 1967 on the verge of certain election as mayor, portions of his following gravitated to various places. Some of his chief lieutenants are said to have suggested a Small E member as candidate, but he declined and endorsed Alioto, who at that point was little known publicly, despite solid duty on the school board and a legal career in antimonopoly law that had made him a multimillionaire.

Alioto thereupon inherited much of McAteer's organization, which included both traditional conservative Democrats and some CDC members. But the main CDC support was and still is behind Congressman Phillip Burton who supported Supervisor Jack Morrison against Alioto. Organized labor, in this town where labor is very important politically, swung from the CDC to back Alioto; the resulting tensions between Burton and Alioto have not yet been resolved. Alioto made the usual swing of ethnic areas, but he worked especially hard and successfully to lure black votes away from Morrison, the expected heir. Thus the mayor drew his support from different factions of the Democratic party—the conservative and usually more affluent Irish, the labor unions, the upper-middle-class intellectuals and the ghetto blacks.

In the Republican party, a conservative-liberal factionalism is more evident. In the last decades the party has lost electoral support gradually (registration is now heavily Democratic), but there is little agreement among their leaders why this is so. One answer might be that young moderates and liberals complain they receive insufficient support from the more conservative and well-heeled party members whose tolerance of deviance from old-line Republicans is nil.

For example, take the cases of John Burton, a liberal Democrat like his brother Phillip, and Caspar Weinberger, a liberal Republican—two young men whom the city sent to the state legislature in different years. Weinberger's career was outstanding (he was voted the best freshman legislator), but his law firm is said to have received little support from Republican clients in the city who were unhappy about the young legislator's occasional straying from the party fold on votes. He later moved to high administrative position under Governor Reagan and then President Nixon. In contrast, Burton is said to have gone to Sacramento on a retainer from a number of unions; his law firm prospered, and there seemed to be more forgiveness from his constituents for his party deviations.

The Republican candidate in the 1967 mayoral race, Harold Dobbs, was a longtime supervisor who had lost once before in this contest. His party was heavily outnumbered, there was little party organization, and his conservative image cost him votes. Indeed, liberal Republican leaders privately reported they backed Alioto, thereby providing him yet another bloc of support. Further, Alioto played the two candidates off against one another, alleging that "a vote for Morrison is a vote for Dobbs," which is to say, Democrats supporting the sure-to-lose Democrat would split the majority, giving it all to Dobbs.

In all this confusion party structure, predictably, has only a paper existence. There is no cadre of precinct or ward workers except that provided by each candidate or, in times past, the CDC. The candidates also do the bulk of their own fund-raising. There is a Central Committee, currently regarded among Democrats as being controlled by Congressman Burton, but no one seems to know why such control is important. In ostensibly nonpartisan elections the committee doesn't endorse candidates; formally this is illegal, but informally there is fear of driving away Republican support. While the committee does take stands on some issues, they are seldom, if ever, publicized. In this world of form without substance—not unlike the smile of Alice's Cheshire cat—the struggles to control the Central Committee seem meaningless, a mark of the politician's propensity to grab any loose marbles lying around.

Quite obviously, however, the lack of meaningful party machinery has done nothing to inhibit the rise of a turbulent local politics. The central issues are not unlike those of any urban area in America. There is a tension between the demands upon government to spend more money and the taxpayers' desire to keep the rates down. Taxes have increased significantly recently; when on the eve of the fall 1969 election citizens were hit by large tax increases, almost every bond issue failed.

Conservation has a special power to arouse San Franciscans because of the city's remarkably beautiful setting. The citizens are peculiarly narcissistic about that beauty, even beyond Oliver Wendell Holmes's observation that "the center of Earth's gravity runs through every small town in America." But then, they have much to be narcissistic about. A poll in late 1969 showed Americans rating San Franciso above all other cities, primarily for its natural beauty.

Local governments' efforts to satisfy different ethnic interests have given a distinctive shape to urban politics all over America, and San Francisco is no exception. With the third highest percentage of foreign-born or foreign-stock population of any city in America (behind New York and Boston), a special part of San Francisco's mystique has been the notion of its tolerance for differing ethnic ways of life. Somehow the flooding into this port from the time of the forty-niners onward has created a tradition of a haven of diversity, an oasis of equal treatment for restless migrants from Malta to Samoa.

But that image of equal treatment is not the reality. The reality is certainly less hollow than in the Mississippi Delta or along the Rio Grande—but equality is still far away. And it certainly wasn't there to begin with. The forty-niners were a bloodthirsty, gold-grubbing lot who believed in equality—among Anglo-Americans. If you were Mexican, Indian or Chinese, and had by some miracle staked out a claim, the odds were excellent that one of those forty-niners would either steal it from you or shoot you for it. This city's subsequent history of tolerance is not all that heartwarming either. Before the turn of the century, one successful mayoral candidate ran on a platform openly advocating violence against the Chinese; Mayor Alioto frequently cites this as evidence of the city's great strides in ethnic amity. One bit of ethnic nastiness that San Francisco does seem to have escaped is the anti-Irish prejudice of the East's Yankee Establishment, possibly because there never was much of that Establishment here.

But refraining from killing one another is not the same thing as tolerance or equality. Today there is a high degree of ethnic enmity, or at least rivalry, mainly because of the persistence of ethnic ties that scholars once thought had been assimilated out of existence. The persistence creates friction for Chinese and Negroes. And possibly the most underplayed story of consequence for the political future of California is the political awakening of the Chicano.

Black, yellow and brown demands for power are new elements in the ethnic politics of San Francisco, but here, as elsewhere, they must operate within the restraining context of more favored ethnic groups—the Irish and Italians. For most of this century the Irish have dominated the politics of the city, and their names are legion in the lists of civil service. In days past, the Byzantine intricacies of San Francisco's government and regulations were passed on as daily fare to Irish children, immensely improving their chances of passing the civil service exams and of maintaining themselves thereafter. Politicians who went to Saint Ignatius High School and thence to the University of San Francisco (both Catholic) joined an "old boys" circuit of influence not unlike that of the private school and Ivy League in the East.

Italian names are becoming somewhat more prominent in city politics, partly because of the success of Joseph Alioto, although he was not the first Italian mayor. A glance at the roster of City Hall clerks and of patrolmen might find the Italian presence looming larger now than it did a quarter century or more ago. But their voice has not become sufficiently dominant to speak of "ethnic succession"—yet.

Special mention should be made in this brief ethnic survey of the position of the Jews of San Francisco, for the city *has* been more open to them than probably any other in America. Their names appear not merely in the sponsorship of cultural, educational and civic groups and causes. They appear also in the politics of both parties, (especially the Democratic), as "fat cat" donors, as behind-the-scene influentials in the Small E and, occasionally, as prominent public officials. None of them when interviewed seems to have a clear reason of why this openness exists. Most trace it to the haste with which San Francisco developed after the gold rush. Many of the now leading Jewish families came here together at about that time. In any event, they are now very nearly the Brahmins of San Francisco. They are still blackballed at some social clubs, but they also support and sit on the boards of Roman Catholic colleges.

In this context of invisible parties and turbulent ethnic politics, the election process is much like the start of those long-distance races; everybody is on his own, eyes straight ahead, a considerable amount of jostling in the pack. Candidates raise their own funds, rarely coalesce with other candidates in a slate, and strive earnestly to reach across party and ethnic lines. With all elections at-large, many candidates for a given office, and no runoff, the impression provided the voter is best characterized by the local practice of slapping posters on buildings, fences and poles. On election day the city's walls are a kaleidoscope of jarring, confusing and possibly self-defeating posters.

One consequence of such partyless politics is reminiscent of what V. O. Key found in his study, *Southern Politics*. Because the party does not bind its candidates to a common program, temporary coalitions of voters support a given candidate but fall away by the next election, thereby rendering impossible any accountability for program. What mandate could be perceived, for example, in the at-large 1965 election of Peter Tamaras for supervisor? An incumbent—and until 1967 most of the supervisors elected were incumbents—he was supported by business, Congressman Burton and Cyril Magnin—conservative, very liberal and moderate liberal. He received the largest vote—60 percent —but this represented only 37 percent of the registered voters, 23 percent of those over 21 and 17.2 percent of the total population. With only small minorities contributing to his election and with a contingent of supporters many of whom hardly speak to one another, how does one measure Supervisor Tamaras's responsibility in the use of his office?

The system emphasized responsiveness, if not responsibility. The major vote-getting device of San Franciscan candidates is to appear before neighborhood groups and ethnic clubs seeking endorsements. Politicians do this in every city, of course, but there are always some groups who are judged not worth battling for. In San Francisco, however, a basic informal rule is that the candidate *must* confront these groups. Night after night he follows an unending sequence of group meetings where he briefly states his qualifications. Sometimes he will have secured the endorsement ahead of time, but he must show up anyway. Once there, as often as not, he is jammed into a reception room to wait his turn, along with the other candidates. It's all rather like freshmen nervously waiting in their rooms on the night when fraternities give out bids. The number of groups is extraordinary and their diversity staggering: ethnics, taxpayers, neighborhood home-owners, conservationists, businessmen, unions and even homosexuals (who are interested in the candidate's sensitivity to civil rights).

If this system encourages responsiveness to local interests, it is questionable whether it also furthers responsibility in the use of power. A candidate cannot be certain what combination of interests most clearly supports him. He may know the region of the votes and he may know which groups endorsed him, but he can't be certain which worked for him and which did not. As the parties have no internal discipline, they cannot provide any clear-cut image of responsibility for the voters and cannot impose a sense of purpose upon their members' task of governance. Even if the parties were to attempt it, the structural obstacles embodied in the city charter are immense.

In 1932 the voters approved a charter whose primary purpose was to prevent widespread corruption. It succeeded admirably. Indeed, the charter divided the power and structure of governance into so many pieces that if officials wanted to be corrupted, the game would hardly be worth the candle. But as charter critics now say, the price for achieving this honesty was to make San Francisco's governors impotent, robbing them of co-ordinated instruments for meeting crucial urban problems as they emerged. The cover of the League of Women Voters' excellent 1967 volume wryly caught the essence of the city's government. A Calder-like mobile is shown with figures frozen in midair but interconnected in inexplicable ways by lines zooming all over the place. A mobile is a thing of beauty, but, as countless observers of the city have complained, "It's a hell of a way to run a railroad."

The charter combines some features of the strong mayor, weak mayor, chief administrative officer and commission forms of governing. To control corruption, members of the legislative Board of Supervisors are elected in off years and at-large in a part-time office for staggered terms. Innumerable boards and commissions, designed to maximize citizen participation—long before the current interest in "participatory democracy"—exercise powers independent of the mayor, except in that he appoints them; some are very responsive to him, however, as the mayor is said to run the police department through the police commission. (Some see these commissions as a throwback to the old vigilante committees of a century ago.) Further, the chief administrative officer (CAO) has limited administrative power; he has no financial or appointive authority; at the same time, however, because he cannot be removed except for serious cause, the CAO is literally appointed for life.

The comptroller has probably the greatest administrative power—all of which leaves the mayor with little formal power short of appointment and budget-making, and even that is limited under a charter that mandates extensive civil service and merit systems. Supervisors are supposed to function exclusively as legislators; indeed, under penalty of law, they cannot advise administrators on the ordinances they originate. Meanwhile, the CAO supervises several city departments, commissions administer yet other functions, and the school board, though appointed by the mayor, is independent of the formal government and of the electorate.

Strangely enough, electoral participation in such a hodge-podge is both expensive and limited. Note that the CAO, comptroller and other administrative officials of considerable power do not stand for election. With long tenure and profound knowledge of the uses of the charter, they may have more real influence than the mayor or supervisors—yet they are virtually untouchable by the electorate. As if in compensation, however, San Francisco's charter offers the citizens 65 elective offices, 18 directly elected at-large and 47 in effect confirmed by the electorate, usually after appointment by the mayor.

But the greatest influence of the electorate lies in the referendum. Every time even the most minor charter change—often only administrative—is required, there must be a referendum. Though only a tiny minority of San Franciscans understand the minutiae of these proposals, at every election they are confronted with 10 to 20 of them. Eugene Lee has concisely indicated the consequences for the political system when

> the charter . . . is full of administrative detail which
> necessitates bringing to the voters countless matters on
> which they cannot and should not be expected to be

properly informed. The politics of charter amendment are dominated by the fact that city elections involve a relatively light turnout, and of those who turn out thousands do not vote on the ballot propositions. Therefore, small groups in the city are able to influence the character of the charter far out of proportion to their numbers.

The referendum might seem an excellent way to work out democracy's basic premises about popular sovereignty, but it creates serious problems for the total polity. The referendum is essentially a method for resolving a conflict, but another and far more frequently used method lies in the process of political parties. In normal party operations the politician, driven by the necessity to construct majorities, strives to ameliorate the sharp edges of intergroup conflict. Usually this means a search for compromise, some broader ground on which competing groups can live. In this process, a compromise requires groups under that party label to work together in order to protect the party's tenure.

But in the absence of parties and with the substitution of the referendum, something else happens. Recent studies by Gerald M. Pomper and by David W. Abbott (the latter on New York's referendum on the civilian review board) argue that this decision-making device polarizes all segments of the public, particularly the ethnic groups. Without any overriding concern to further the political party's control of government and without the party agents moving among competing groups searching for a viable compromise, each group feels more alone, insecure and hence hostile and suspicious of suggestions that it modify its views. The use of party to ameliorate group conflict has its vices, too, as even the casual student of contemporary urban affairs must know. Yet the reformist urge to democratize public decision-making by decentralizing it should not be accepted without recognition that its price is a heightened polarization and perhaps a deadening immobility.

In a highly pluralistic nation, the accumulated price of such fractionated decision-making is considerable. In a highly pluralistic city such as San Francisco, the price has become *non*decision-making. When successful policy outcome rests necessarily upon the agreement of so many disparate private groups and public authorities, the power of one component to block any action is magnified. Over time, consequently, only minor policy adjustments are possible, and it is highly doubtful whether these add up to an adequate response to deep and widespread community problems. Instead, the bulk of public policy-making is done by civil servants beyond the reach of the electorate. Each of these functionaries can affect only small sections of the government, but cumulatively their little decisions comprise the totality of public policy. Moreover, the central drift of the pattern of these decisions can best be characterized as nondecision. And the decision not to act has as much public consequence as the decision to act.

What San Francisco has, then, is government by clerks. That feature of urban life is not distinctive to "The City," of course, but the clerical power is enhanced by the relative absence of instruments for maintaining clerical responsibility. The political party, not being there, cannot perform that function. Civil service or charter status makes for immunity from election or recall. Indeed, the city workers' union is a sufficient power in itself to affect electoral outcomes for offices and referenda.

The immunity of the clerks seems an invitation to public corruption. Yet in recent decades this has not been the case at all. The one recent instance of corruption, that of the city assessor, involved relatively small amounts of public money for himself, and $9 million has since been recovered from favored taxpayers. Far more characteristic are the CAO and controller. Although removed from the electorate, everyone regards them as possessing a high degree of competence and probity. While this government of clerks may be incapacitated, it is certainly not dishonest.

An experienced bureaucrat once highlighted the problem by an example that would be ridiculous if it weren't true. If a scrap of paper blew in front of the City Hall steps, it could not be swept up until a jurisdictional decision was made as to the appropriate agency. If found on the sidewalk, it would belong to the street-cleaning department; if on the stairs, to the building superintendent; and if on the lawn, to the agency for recreation and parks.

What of the mayor? The position is what he makes it by the force of his character and personality, but he has very little power at his best. Among his roles is that of Chief Greeter for the city, and given the flow of the world's notables through this port (film companies are shooting all over town now), he could well fill his time. If he has higher ambitions, he could play the role of Rising Politico, spending a lot of time in Sacramento or Washington or other watering places of politicians. The two roles are not exclusive, of course, although no San Francisco mayor has gone to higher state or national office since the days of "Sunny Jim" Rolph in the 1920s. Earl Warren, non-Californians should note, came from Alameda County across the Bay.

Joseph Alioto entered office with a splash, clearly trying to rise above these limited roles—without, however, ignoring them. His advisors report him as wearing a multiplicity of hats—ceremonial, public relations officer, carrier of some authority, concerned about crucial urban problems. Keenly aware of the charter and political limitations of his office, Alioto tries to use to the utmost that power which may ultimately be the prime one for all executives, public and private. This is the power to persuade.

People close to the mayor say he approaches his work

with several basic notions of the community. He sees it as a matrix of pluralist conflict in which every day a host of issues—usually small—agitates the body politic and in which invisible groups are constantly winning and losing. The manipulation of these issues is necessary to enhance the mayor's power, even when the most he can do formally is get the contenders to sit down and talk. In this view, the mayor's office requires more legislative than executive work, more bargaining among equals than issuing authoritative demands.

This might seem to make him powerless, because not controlling a hierarchy of powers in the Weberian model, he must haggle and bargain. Instead, the mayor's influence over the outcome of policy conflicts rests on his ability to persuade others to find a satisfactory compromise or set of trade-offs among contending groups. Such is the potential in the mayor's office of this city—and perhaps of most, if not all, cities in America.

But for this model to work effectively, the mayor needs not merely persuasiveness but information. Alioto is said to have developed a personal network of supporters in many commissions and departments who provide information on happenings in their bailiwicks. Other mayors here did not do this. Newsmen form another part of that network of information. The mayor's flamboyant style makes good copy, and the press often returns the favor in its kind. The intelligence network provides him not merely with data on what is or may be happening and on who wants what; it also allows him to communicate to the government and community the image he desires—as one advisor put it, that of "a man of energy and class."

As a part of his concern to use the office's potential more fully, Alioto is said to have wanted to break out of the "City Hall syndrome" of problem-solving, that is, the usual practice of getting the bureaucrats together to discuss a new problem. Although little emerged from this practice, it did provide newspaper copy which gave the impression that something was being done. Instead, Mayor Alioto looks to other experts to contribute to his decisions. He actively seeks out the views of special groups. He has made special efforts to reach out to the black community and to create an image of helpfulness. But to ask for advice is not the same as being able to translate it into hard policy.

Other means have to be found for that. Thus, in the final year of the Johnson administration, as a solid Humphrey supporter, Alioto was poking into every crevice of the federal government for funds for community projects. While successful at times in Washington, he was often stymied by agencies and interests back home. The failure to obtain a Model Cities program occurred primarily because city agencies failed to meet federal deadlines—despite Alioto's urgings. Private business provides only a fraction of the summer or permanent jobs needed to attack hard-core poverty among the young. His supporters claim, however, that he sought help for some city problems from business contacts made during his legal career.

Yet another force of possible use in translating public preferences into public policies lies in his reputation as a Rising Politico. From the day of his election, Alioto has been surrounded by excited expectations that he would go on to higher things politically. This possibility of increased eminence may have attracted some of the independent power-holders of city government who simply like to be associated with future governors or senators. But this Rising Politico role exacted a price—the time and energy it took away from the city. Administrators are more likely to move when the mayor leans on them persuasively and continually, a likelihood diminished when part of his time must be spent considering his political future. Whatever this role may do for the mayor in the future, it limits his present power to persuade.

As we have indicated, that power is a fragile thing— in president or mayor—and this has certainly been the case with Alioto. *Look* magazine's allegations in 1969 of his supposed connections with the Mafia dealt him a serious blow. Following close upon this attack, the Republican attorney general of the state of Washington claimed that Alioto had improperly split fees with a former Democratic attorney general in some utility cases Alioto had handled for that state. The mayor promptly and energetically rebutted both charges, in the first mounting a multimillion dollar damage suit and in the second opening all his books for examination to underline his claim that nothing illegal or unethical was involved.

But state polls showed that his political future had been hurt. It was tough enough as it was. Seemingly intent upon the governor's chair, he already faced two major obstacles—Jess Unruh's desire for the job and Ronald Reagan's immense popularity. In January 1970 Alioto declined to run, and by June 1970 he was clearly intent on running for mayor again in 1971.

The role of Rising Politico, then, probably offers little to help a mayor in his efforts to strengthen his persuasiveness and to impose some programmatic unity on the city. The fragmentation of power makes it difficult to construct a convincing record as administrator which could be trumpeted to the state. The resources needed to work hard at future eminence diminish his influence in the city administration. Setbacks in his political aspirations may well diminish it further.

I take time for this consideration of Alioto's administration not because he is one of the more charismatic mayors in the city's history to have adopted the role of Chief Persuader, but because with all his local popularity, energy, publicity and serious effort, the problems of the city remain unsolved. Part of the reason for this rests with the structural limitations imposed by the charter. Another rests with the swirl of urban issues for whose resolution he has few resources. Ethnic conflict is increasing, and the militants in each of these groups become more dominant, more resistant to compromise, more irreconcilable. The housing shortage becomes more severe, the tax load heavier, and discontent with the nature of emerging urban life more evident in more segments of the public.

The point is not, however, that all this is the mayor's fault but that these problems are increasing in spite of, not because of, the mayor's effort and that this condition afflicts every mayor in America today. Most American mayors find it difficult to provide the leadership and the resources to cure an appalling list of urban ills. Urban reformists, in their drive for administrative unification and centralization, pay little attention to the need for strengthening the mayor's power to form coalitions of interests to meet major urban problems. That function is rather left to the vagaries of mayoral character and temperament.

Where then does one find such an integrative force? San Francisco's mayor, whoever holds the office, may only be the least equipped of the lot to provide political unification. And yet leadership for these tasks emerges from no other single group or combination of groups in the community. The business influence of "the Downtowners" and the Chamber of Commerce has waned recently as other groups' voices are being heard. Unions, particularly the powerful city workers, consider proposals for the mobilization of power to meet current problems as a threat to the interests currently vested in the charter. Ethnic groups have eyes only for their own kind. The major corporations, whose gleaming—and often ugly—buildings increasingly fill the downtown, are more interested in defending their interests at the state, national and international levels.

Meanwhile, the local government with its multiple points of seeming access to the city's pluralist society does not provide access to those claiming new needs and new problems. Against these the government is insulated, droning on, with little effective leadership.

In November 1969 almost every major element of the city publicly attested to the validity of the preceding analysis by swamping an effort to reform the city charter. Sixty-three percent opposed reform, and probably only the League of Women Voters supported it. Each of the other major groups in the community found some portion of the revision so seriously threatening that they advised their members to vote "No." The reforms sought to strengthen the mayor's office, unify the commissions' powers and in other ways combine the resources of local government to meet the issues of 1970 and not those of 1932. It failed, reform leaders resigned, and the event explains much of the failure of contemporary reform proposals for urban government.

These proposals have traditionally emphasized upper-middle-class values of efficiency and rationality. These values are to be maximized by structures designed to centralize power in visible positions filled by professionally trained personnel. The ideal is reflected in the city manager government concept, where a professional isolated from ostensibly grubby political influences is set free to administer efficiently the corporation of government, much in the way the business corporation's managing director operates. But such a proposal is seldom accepted in America's largest cities; none over 800,000 uses it, and the bigger ones adopted it three or more decades ago. The reason lies in another set of values embedded in prevailing institutions which reflect the very pluralistic and ethnic composition of these big cities.

The city workers of San Francisco furnish a prime exam-

ple of these other values. Their interest lies not merely in a
job but in the identity, success and hopes of an ethnic
group. When persons of other ethnic identities talk reform,
any appeal to general values of rationality and responsibility seems merely a camouflage to those threatened. Con-
versely, when the attacks on special interest come from
emergent ethnic groups levying new claims for a shred of
the resources from the body politic, ethnic prejudices and
political principles merge in an indistinguishable fashion.

Those protected are not merely ethnic groups, of course.
Taxpayers fear changes, although as one looks at the taxpayers' plight around the country it's hard to see how reform could squeeze them any harder than they already are.
Business groups, used to a special and favorable connection with the licensing and taxing power of cities, find
some administrative reform proposals equally threatening.
Protectors of a particular cultural institution, such as the
museums, warily eye reformist notions about unification
of the control of all cultural programs. City workers, used
to having their way on wages and pensions in an electorate
where their own vote bulks large, see nothing but loss if
such decisions are to be made legislatively.

If reformists in San Francisco still have hope, their best
strategy may lie in publicizing how unbearable are the
costs of maintaining the status quo, how really unprotected
they are under this system. When citizens defeated completion of the Embarcadero Freeway a few years ago, they
demonstrated a widespread refusal to accept the costs of
the loss of beauty just to save the time of motorists. Although San Francisco and other American cities have not
yet accepted it, there is however another cost—widespread
but subtle—arising from the system's inability to respond
to critical physical, social and economic needs. All San
Franciscans have this in common—they pay for systematic
failure to respond by higher taxes, deteriorating environ-

ment, rising crime rate, worse living conditions, traffic congestion and the rest.

All pay for this, but the poor pay more than most, a different kind of regressive "tax" system, when one conceives taxes as something more than what tax assessors levy. Taxed in this fashion but unable to move a system toward some kind of tax equity, the disadvantaged cannot, like their ancestors, withhold taxes and cry, "No taxation without representation!" Smog, congestion, crime and sweatshops cannot be withheld. One can endure them or strike out blindly. In the latter case, the city may yet pay for its failure to recognize a present cost common to all.

Reform may occur in another, more macabre way. Disaster often generates change. The commission form of government was born out of a hurricane in Galveston a half century ago. Reforms at the national level have often if not predominantly proceeded from large-scale disaster, as witness something as major as the New Deal legislation or as minor as the Drug Control Act of 1962. Unfortunately for reformists, one cannot stage a disaster, so for most American cities the strategy is meaningless. However, the city of San Francisco sits on the major earthquake line of the San Andreas fault, and geologists anticipate an earthquake any day or month or year—but soon. When one imagines this city's little mobile of a government trying to cope with the effects of such a cataclysm, he can only shudder. But one result will surely be that dangling figures will fall. In that case, by one of the ironies which delight intellectuals, that Nature which has made the Bay so beautiful in the past may in the future help make local government effective.

Such speculation should not be regarded as a signal to the League of Women Voters and other reformers to set off dynamite blasts underground. It does suggest, however, the extraordinary tenacity of the government which has become so adapted to San Francisco's pluralist community. A less drastic strategy for meeting reformists' definition of crisis may be turning toward the federal government. Federal monies provide at least one kind of resource for building new power bases for groups formerly disadvantaged. This may be in rural Mississippi (as I have found) or in the depths of the Oakland ghettos (as Aaron Wildavsky is finding). Traditional groups have their power bases in the local charter or in traditional ways of operating, but emergent groups may find their power base in yet another source, the federal government. Yet another player will then have been added to the urban team but at the cost of a drastic diminution of the role of city government in policy-making that affects its citizens.

It is partly a question of where pluralist pressures arising out of the city are to have their focus. Reformists call for strengthening local government so that the myriad of needs arising from the community can be met and handled there. Others argue that this strengthening cannot take place because the city's vested power bastions can fight off new demands. They want to bypass the city and go to Washington to focus pressure, for the group denied access to local government can achieve power through some national program. That merely leads to another question, how the "locals" and the "feds" are going to agree what decisions should be made.

Federal intervention to assist groups now disadvantaged seems more likely to work than efforts to rearrange the total structure through charter reform. If the former does work, American federalism will once again have demonstrated its extraordinary versatility in adapting to new demands. In such a fashion, too, the contention of political pluralists may find some vindication, even though federal programs to date have been far too limited to do more than begin the process of helping disadvantaged groups. In this context, San Francisco provides a severe test of the adaptability of federalism. Its fragmentation of governmental power and structure, its absence of party organization and processes for welding the seams of a pluralist system, its government by clerks which enfolds in its crevices a variety of special interests—all provide a politics of pluralism with a vengeance.

But, like almost everything else in San Francisco, it is fascinating to gaze at.

Store Front Lawyers
in San Francisco

JEROME E. CARLIN

A United States district court on April 22, 1968 invalidated California's residency requirements for persons seeking public assistance. Previously, applicants had to be residents of the state for at least one year before they could become eligible for benefits. According to the *San Francisco Chronicle* of April 25:

> The Reagan Administration will try to overturn last week's landmark Federal Court decision. . . . Health and Welfare Director Spencer Williams said the decision would add another 24 million dollars to welfare costs, and adds about 6,900 families and 12,000 other individuals to the welfare rolls.

On December 28, 1968 the *New York Times* printed the following story datelined San Francisco:

POOR WIN VICTORY IN A HOUSING SUIT

COURT HALTS COAST RENEWAL UNTIL

RESIDENTS BACK PLAN

A Federal Court has halted the funding of a $100 million

125

urban renewal project here with a decision that is expected to affect similar projects across the country and aid the poor in establishing legal rights for themselves. The court order prohibits the Department of Housing and Urban Development from supplying additional funds for the project until an acceptable plan has been approved for relocating uprooted families. . . . In taking the action to court, the Western Addition community group was [represented] by the San Francisco Neighborhood Legal Assistance Foundation. . . .

On August 12, 1969 the following appeared on the front page of the *Chronicle:*

BAY JUDGE ORDERS BOOST IN WELFARE

More money must be paid in rent allotments to people in the biggest welfare program in San Francisco and Alameda Counties, a Superior Court judge ruled here yesterday. Judge Alvin E. Weinberger further ordered the State Department of Social Welfare to take steps that will produce another increase in rent money across the State in a few months time.

He acted in a law suit brought by the San Francisco Neighborhood Legal Assistance Foundation on behalf of all persons receiving Aid to Families with Dependent Children (AFDC) in the two counties. Foundation lawyers charged that most AFDC clients are getting a monthly rent allotment less than the actual rent they are paying. Under State law, the Department's standards for rent must insure "safe, healthful housing." And the Department's own regulations require that its rent stanards be based on "current actual costs for housing."

Judge Weinberger said the state and counties must live up to their own laws and regulations. . . .

The total sum required statewide would be $19 million per year. . . . This would pay the actual rent. How much more would be required after the Department hearings, to pay for safe, healthful housing is a matter of dispute. But the total increase could reach $50 million.

These have been some of the more newsworthy activities of a new type of professional organization. The San Francisco Neighborhood Legal Assistance Foundation is a federally financed, community-controlled legal service agency which has been aggressively advocating the rights of the poor since it began operation in Ocotober 1966. It is one of about 300 agencies throughout the United States funded by the Office of Economic Opportunity (OEO) to deliver more effective legal services to the nation's poor.

Since the foundation has probably gone farther than almost any of the other legal service agencies in carrying out this mandate and has served as a model for many other programs in the United States, it may be instructive to examine what it set out to accomplish, the extent to which it was able to achieve its objectives, and the problems it encountered. One of the most important issues that emerges from such an inquiry is the apparent incompatibility of the two principal goals of the organization: control by the client community and institutional change.

Having participated in the creation of the foundation, and having served as its head for the first three years of its existence, I will be presenting an insider's view that may well be biased and self-serving. I trust that my training as a sociologist and lawyer will serve to curb any major excesses.

The foundation is a private, nonprofit corporation with a governing board consisting of representatives of the local bar associations, law schools and the poverty community. The bylaws require that a majority of the board members be selected by the five poverty areas in San Francisco and that the board must also have a majority of attorneys. This is accomplished by having each poverty area select at least one lawyer representative. The board hires the coordinator, who is the chief executive officer of the foundation, and the directing attorney (chief counsel) for each of the five neighborhood law offices. The coordinator is responsible for carrying out the overall policies of the organization (which are determined by him and the board), for allocating resources among the various offices and departments and for hiring and supervising administrative and legal staff at the headquarters office (Main Office) of the foundation. Each chief counsel hires and fires his own staff of attorneys, secretaries, law students and aides.

In the fall of 1969 there were more than 120 paid staff persons working at the foundation including 50 full-time attorneys and about 30 part-time law students. In addition, about 25 law students and 10 social work students spent varying amounts of time at the foundation for credit under faculty supervision. Numerous private attorneys, on a volunteer basis, interview clients in the evening at a neighborhood office, make court appearances on default divorces or perform other services.

The staff attorneys are generally young—about a fourth came to the foundation right out of law school (mostly through the OEO-funded Reginald Heber Smith Fellowship and VISTA programs); only about a third had at least four years of practice experience before joining the foundation. Most attended top-ranking law schools; approximately a third graduated from an Ivy League law school (Harvard, Yale or Columbia). One out of four foundation attorneys is from a minority group; there are nine black lawyers.

The yearly budget of the foundation is over a million dollars, practically all of which comes from OEO in the form of an annual grant channeled through the local poverty agency, the Economic Opportunity Council of San Francisco (EOC). Although the foundation must deal both with OEO and EOC, it is essentially the former, and particularly the Legal Services Division within OEO, that has played the principal role in articulating and enforcing general guidelines for the foundation (and other legal service agencies) and evaluating performance.

OEO seeks to shape and control programs and promote certain national objectives, not only through the funding process, but also by means of nationwide training programs, research and back-up centers and fellowship programs that place bright young law school graduates in funded agencies. Many foundation lawyers (particularly those working in the Main Office) maintain close ties with other poverty lawyers throughout the country by taking an active part in these OEO programs as well as meetings of the National Legal Aid and Defender Association (which has become largely dominated by OEO lawyers) and other newly developed associations of poverty lawyers. In the national poverty law movement, OEO's Legal Services (in alliance with the American Bar Association, if not all or even most state and local bar associations) continues to play a leading role, giving solid support (with only few lapses) to program goals generally more advanced than most funded agencies are wiling or able to realize.

Every month over a thousand new clients come into the five neighborhood offices of the foundation. A large majority of the clients are seeing a lawyer for the first time, most are on welfare,and half are in families with an annual income of less than $3,000 a year. About 15 percent of the clients are referred out—mainly to private attorneys or the public defender—because they fall above the foundation's income standard or they have a fee-producing or criminal case. The largest number of clients (about 30 percent) want help with a family problem, and half of these are seeking a divorce. The next biggest group are those having problems with administrative agencies: welfare, unemployment insurance, social security, immigration and naturalization (the bulk of the cases in the Chinatown Office) and the draft. Problems with landlords and merchants (and their collection agents) each constitute about 15 percent of the cases.

A major portion of the family cases, including all divorce matters, are referred to the Domestic Relations Unit, located at the Main Office, for more expeditious handling. This innovation has been adopted by a great many other programs and has contributed significantly to reducing the overall time and resources that need be devoted to this largely routine service.

The Main Office also houses a legal staff handling a limited number of cases that are selected because they raise major poverty issues in public housing, welfare, urban renewal and more recently in the consumer area. The cases are referred to the staff from community organization or neighborhood office lawyers. In time the Main Office attorneys have become specialists in the particular areas in which they work, in contrast with most attorneys in the neighborhood offices who, given the diversity of legal problems they have to deal with and the relatively little time they have to give any particular case, remain essentially general practitioners.

The foundation was largely the creation of Charles Baumbach, a politically astute young lawyer who put together a coalition of white militant lawyers (primarily Jewish) and minority professionals (mainly black) who held positions in the local poverty power structure. The founders had a common cause in their insistence on neighborhood control of legal services.

For the lawyer-founders, community control was in part a means of negating control by the organized bar which they felt would be opposed to a more aggressive form of advocacy, one that would seek to use the law as an instrument of social change. The lawyers were also committed to altering the conventional power relation between the poor and the agencies that purport to serve them. Community control would create new opportunities for the poor to participate in determining agency policy and decisions, and this principle should also apply to legal service programs for the poor, or so it was felt.

For their part, the neighborhood poverty leaders had just fought and won a battle with the mayor for majority control of the EOC by representatives from the "target" areas, and they wanted control of the legal services component as well. Their reasons were complex: in part they were simply extending the demand for self-determination; in part they had learned to resent the paternalism and insensitivity of traditional legal aid. But there was also a desire to expand a new power base by gaining control over jobs, services and other rewards for constituents.

Majority control of the Board of Directors by representatives of the poor was one expression of the neighborhood leaders' insistence on community control. Another was the very considerable autonomy given the neighborhood offices. The local leaders envisioned that each of the poverty areas would in effect have its own law firm. The chief counsel of the neighborhood office was to be selected by the board, rather than the coordinator, and it was assumed that the representatives on the board of a particular neighborhood would have primary say in choosing the attorney to head "their" office. Also, limiting the powers of coordinator would, it was hoped, minimize racial and ethnic jealousies —given the ethnic mix of San Francisco's poverty areas— and provide a hedge against a bad director.

Community control was the unifying issue for the lawyers and neighborhood leaders who established the foundation. It was also the major issue in the foundation's sometimes bitter struggle with the legal establishment in San Francisco. After a year-long battle, the foundation won a stunning victory when it finally convinced OEO officials to fund it rather than the bar-supported Legal Aid Society of San Francisco. The foundation became the first OEO-funded legal service agency in the United States with majority control by representatives of the poverty community.

Although the neighborhood leaders expressed no particular views regarding the content of the legal program, the lawyer-founders had some very strong ideas about it. These ideas were derived from an analysis of traditional legal aid and some conceptions about law and social change. The lawyers wanted to create an agency that would not only provide remedial assistance to individual clients (albeit in a more sympathetic and aggressive fashion than legal aid), but would also work toward altering conditions that keep the poor powerless and victims of injustice. This aim was based in part upon a recognition of the impossibility, with limited resources, of handling more than a small fraction of the problems urgently calling for legal assistance, and the necessity, therefore, of a more "wholesale" approach. It rested also on the understanding that, as Jan Howard, Sheldon Messinger and I wrote in 1966,

the legal problems of the poor . . . characteristically arise from systematic abuses embedded in the operation of various public and private agencies, affecting large numbers of similarly situated individuals. Effective solution of the problems may require the lawyer to direct his attention away from a particular claim or grievance to the broader interests and policies at stake, and away from the individual client to a class of clients, in order to challenge more directly and with greater impact certain structural sources of injustice.

Very generally speaking, we came in time to conceive of our mission in this way: to find leverage points in the system to bring about a redistribution of power and income more favorable to the poor. Two general approaches were developed: strategic advocacy and economic development. Under the first, we sought to enter into the variety of forums where the law is made and administered, to facilitate the development of new rights in areas where the law was vague or clearly biased against the poor, or to enforce existing law favorable to the poor which had remained unimplemented (e.g., enforcement of health and safety provisions of the housing code, prohibitions against fraud and misrepresentation in sale of consumer goods).

To a remarkable extent, it appeared that "the system" —be it welfare, urban renewal, private slum housing or the garment industry in Chinatown—could not operate successfully without breaking the law: the cost of compliance is generally greater than the operators of the system are willing to pay, expecially since those most likely to be hurt have been least likely to complain. Consequently, we hoped that vigorous law enforcement might serve not only to redistribute income, but also to mount sufficient pressure to change the system.

The test for the efficacy of such activity was whether it would result in increasing the income or political bargaining power of a substantial number of poor persons. Litigation (with an emphasis on class suits) and administrative and legislative advocacy were the principal tools. In time, however, we learned that these measures, particularly court cases, by themselves were frequently ineffective unless combined with the mobilization of political support in the middle class as well as poverty communities.

By means of the second general approach we sought to promote entrepreneurial activity among ghetto residents. This came later and remained a subsidiary strategy.

Whatever else the foundation may have achieved, it gained a reputation in the community of being a tough advocate for the poor, of being willing to take on any and all opponents—police department, Housing Authority, United States Army, welfare deparment, used-car dealers, Redevelopment Agency, City Hall, board of education. In a skit presented at the Bar Association of San Francisco Annual Ball (December 1968), the following, written by an attorney member, was sung to the tune of "Glowworm":

We're from Neighborhood Legal Assistance
We encourage draft resistance
Nasty landlords are our nemesis
We keep tenants on the premises
We give deadbeats our protection
To frustrate any debt collection
The laws we use are not on your shelf
'Cause we make them up ourself

We soon recognized the importance of publicity in building a reputation: it has been said that we won more cases at press conferences than in the courts. We published our own newsletter which reached several thousand persons, mostly private attorneys in San Francisco, with reports of our more important and more interesting cases. We also made it a point to get our cases into the press. Some idea of the coverage, and the developing image, may be seen in the following:

In one of the most unusual cases handled by the Foundation in recent weeks, 20 year old Ted Townsend, who had been held for three months in the Presidio stockade as a suspected deserter, was freed after his Neighborhood Legal Assistance attorney pointed out . . .(*San Francisco Progress,* August 24, 1967).

A poverty program lawyer has filed a complaint with the Public Utilities Commission, seeking to end Pacific Telephone's $25 deposit requirement for certain new customers. (*Chronicle,* December 16, 1967).

The Neighborhood Legal Assistance Foundation filed a suit that seeks to prevent San Francisco policemen from carrying guns while off duty (*Chronicle*, November 9, 1968).

The San Francisco Neighborhood Legal Assistance Foundation has fired another salvo at the State Department of Social Welfare. (*Examiner*, June 27, 1968).

The unit [the Main Office legal staff] is illustrative both of the length to which the young attorneys in Legal Assistance will go to attempt to help their clients and of the crusading idealism of the men who operate it. (*Examiner*, October 9, 1968).

The Neighborhood Legal Assistance Foundation is seeking a breakthrough in labor practices to make unions more responsive to the needs of their members, especially minority group members with language and cultural problems. (*Argonant*, October 26, 1968).

The San Francisco Neighborhood Legal Assistance Foundation has joined the legal fight against Rudolph Ford, the Daley City car dealer. (*Examiner*, January 14, 1969).

A San Francisco draftee who couldn't get anybody to listen to him finally was heard by a Federal judge who ordered the army to discharge the youth. . . . After a year Bibbs got his story to . . . an attorney with the Neighborhood Legal Assistance Foundation who filed a federal court suit and got Bibbs discharged. (*Chronicle*, March 12, 1969).

A quiet little war has been going on between the San Francisco Neighborhood Legal Assistance Foundation and the state over welfare recipients' rights. . . . (*Chronicle*, March 17, 1969).

Realtor Walter H. Shorenstein was accused yesterday [in a suit filed by the San Francisco Neighborhood Legal Assistance Foundation] of using his position as president of the Recreation and Park Commission to push the destruction of the International Hotel. (*Chronicle*, March 28, 1969).

Our reputation gave us needed leverage in dealing with landlords, merchants, collection agencies, used-car dealers and public agency officials. Often a phone call was all that was necessary; people knew that we meant business and would follow through—indeed we enraged many slumlords' attorneys, who accused us (sometimes in letters to their congressmen) of using taxpayers' money to harass them.

In assessing the clout we developed it must be said that we have primarily benefited particular clients for whom we have been able to get a better deal in bargaining with merchants, landlords, welfare officials and others. Although often gratifying for the lawyer and his client, the benefits are generally remedial and short-lived—very little is basically changed. Housing is a good example. In three years we probably handled at least 4,000 individual cases involving some kind of landlord-tenant dispute. We undoubtedly brought some solace and relief to many individual tenants by delaying an eviction or forcing a landlord to make some repairs. Nevertheless, in those same three years the housing situation for poor people in San Francisco has become a great deal worse. The stock of low-income housing has been further reduced through public and private renewal programs. If plans for the latest renewal project in the Yerba Buena District are not changed, there will be approximately 4,000 fewer units in the city, which means more doubling up or worse, because there are virtually no vacancies among low-income units. The bulk of the housing available to the poor is substandard (at least 60,000 units have been so labeled officially), and is deteriorating further. The waiting list for public housing went up to 5,000, at which point the Housing Authority stopped adding names. Rents have gone up with the decline in the housing stock and increasing taxes—in some areas they have doubled in the past few years. Against this background it might appear as though the foundation had made the process a little more humane without having any effect on the underlying machinery. But that is not quite the case.

There are two areas—redevelopment and welfare—in which we have made at least a small dent in the system, which may well mark the beginning of an even greater impact.

In surveying the general housing situation for the poor in San Francisco, it was clear that top priority had to be placed on preventing any further reduction in the stock of low-income housing. The principal offender in San Francisco, as in other parts of the United States, has been the federal urban renewal program administered through local redevelopment agencies. This program has proceeded on the understanding that there would be no enforcement of those provisions of the Federal Housing Act which require that persons displaced from a project area be relocated into safe, decent and sanitary housing at rents they can afford. If these provisions were to be enforced, then the renewal program would have to go into the business building low-income housing—and this it has never been willing or able to do. As a result, the program has produced a drastic net decline in housing for the poor and has substantially worsened slum conditions.

In 1966 redevelopment was on the move again in San Francisco after nearly a two-year lull caused by the voters' approval of the anti-fair housing Proposition 14. The Redevelopment Agency was eager to proceed with its plans to demolish approximately 4,500 dwelling units of predominently low-cost housing in the Western Addition, thereby displacing close to 10,000 persons—mostly poor and black. Failure of the agency to comply with the relocation provisions of the Federal Housing Act would provide, we hoped, the necessary leverage to challenge the project. (Not only was the relocation plan patently deficient—given San Francisco's unbelievably tight low-income housing market and the absence of any provisions for constructing new housing for displaces—but it turned out that the Department of Housing and Urban Development (HUD) had been honoring agency requisitions for financing the project without having first given its approval of the agency's relocation plan—a clear and gross violation of federal law.) The major obstacle that we faced was the fact that the courts had, unfortunately, refused to monitor federal urban renewal programs on behalf of project residents, on the theory that persons whose homes were being destroyed did not have sufficient stake in the outcome of litigation to give them standing to sue and that such suits involved technical matters too complex for the courts to get into. Even though public officials might be violating the law to the grievous detriment of thousands of poor residents forced out of their homes into even worse circumstances, the courts refused to open their doors to hear these complaints. The principle hurdle, then, was the court itself. Before anything else could be done we had to establish for our clients a most basic right—the right to be heard before a judicial tribunal.

A year and a day after the suit was filed in conjunction with the NAACP Legal Defense Fund—and 16 months after filing an administrative protest with HUD—the court finally reached a decision on the jurisdictional question: it found that our clients had standing to challenge the legality of the agency's relocation plan and issued a preliminary injunction bringing the renewal project in the Western Addition to a grinding halt. This was clearly a landmark decision; it finally brought the federal renewal program under the scrutiny of judicial review, and for the first time in the United States a renewal project had been stopped in midstream.

The case had been brought on behalf of the Western Addition Community Organization (WACO), a federation of grass roots neighborhood organizations, put together a couple of years earlier by a Student Nonviolent Coordinating Committee organizer to fight the second round of redevelopment in the Western Addition (the first round had been decisively lost—only a handful of families out of the many thousands previously residing in the area ever returned). As a result of the court victory, WACO and the residents of the project area were at last given a voice in the decisions and plans so vitally affecting their lives—both in the sense of having gained entrée into the court and also by establishing a viable bargaining position with the Redevelopment Agency. Although the injunction was later dissolved by the court, the Redevelopment Agency had been significantly shaken—and a new and broader-based coalition emerged in the Western Addition which, under agreement with the agency, became an official participant in the renewal process.

Pressure on the Redevelopment Agency has been kept up as projects begin to move in other areas. The Yerba Buena project, which calls for the destruction of 4,000 housing units to make way for a new commercial complex, was also challenged by the foundation in a federal court suit. The clients, who are generally old as well as poor, have literally no place to go. The fight with the Redevelopment Agency, particularly in Yerba Buena, brought the foundation into a head-on confrontation with the San Francisco power structure, and the pressure began to mount, especially from City Hall. Nevertheless, the political alliances that had been forged in support of our clients' interests—including our allies among respectable middle-class groups and civic organizations—held firm.

And once again, and far more rapidly than before, a federal court order was issued temporarily halting relocation of residents.

What then have we accomplished? We have at least slowed down the rate of destruction of low-income housing by public and private agencies. (By saving the International Hotel, which houses the remnant of the Filipino community in San Francisco, from demolition by private developers, we were able to extend some of the principles established in the WACO case into the private sector.) We have also helped fashion a legal-political force that the Redevelopment Agency and the city power structure will have to bargain with in determining housing policies for San Francisco. And we have provided hard evidence that in the area of redevelopment the arbitrary exercise of public power by local authorities and the federal government can be checked.

The other area in which the foundation has made some progress in its goal of institutional change is welfare. To begin with, we have enabled many more poor people to obtain public assistance: at least 60,000 people became eligible to receive welfare benefits as a result of our suit that invalidated California's residency requirement. We also prevented the cutoff of close to 2,000 needy persons from general assistance as an economy move by the San Francisco Department of Social Services. The foundation, moreover, has won several court decisions which, if and when they are implemented, will substantially increase dollar benefits to recipients. In the *Ivy* case the Superior Court ordered that rent allotments for AFDC recipients in San Francisco and Alameda counties be raised immediately to cover actual rentals (this will add about $19 million when extended state-wide) and that a new list of rent allotments be issued reflecting the cost of safe and sanitary housing as required by state law (and this could add at least $30 million more). In the *Nesbitt* case (which we brought with the Alameda County Legal Aid Society), the court held that the state Department of Social Welfare was violating recent state and federal regulations which, as an encouragement to seek employment, exempt a certain portion of the earnings of working recipients in calculating their welfare grant. As a result, it was estimated that working recipients were getting approximately $30 a month less than they were entitled to. Enforcement of this decision could increase payments to recipients by about $9 million. In the *Kaiser* case, also brought with the Alameda County Legal Aid Society, the federal court declared unconstitutional a California statute placing a ceiling on the amount of money that could be granted to AFDC recipients, a ceiling that was actually lower than the state's own determination of the minimum required for subsistence.

Insofar as we have sought to increase the amount of money going to welfare recipients, we appear to have been successful in adding somewhere between $50 and $100 million—this includes the $25 to $30 million a year estimated increase in welfare costs resulting from the residency decision. Not bad for a $3 million investment in legal services in San Francisco.

These figures, however, may turn out to be something less than firm. The state has many options to limit, delay or in other ways frustrate the carrying out of the courts' decisions. The state Department of Social Welfare can engage us in lengthy appellate proceedings, it can adopt new regulations to reduce the cost of particular decisions, it can simply refuse to comply with court orders (as it is now doing in the rent case), or the legislature may change the state law that was the basis for the court victory.

It became necessary, therefore, for us to attend to these other arenas. This required not only our presence at hearings and meetings of state and county welfare bodies and appearances before legislative committees, but the mobilizing of welfare recipients and others to bring pressure to bear on administrative and legislative decision-makers. Formation of an active city-wide welfare rights organization was achieved in part through a series of welfare advocates' classes conducted in various neighborhoods by the foundation's welfare specialists.

Pressure from the poverty community has been fairly effective in San Francisco, much less effective in Sacramento. Effectiveness in Sacramento requires not only state-wide organization, but support from other than welfare recipients, and it is certainly questionable whether this support will be forthcoming when most middle-class voters feel that more money for welfare inevitably comes out of their pockets. Nevertheless, an important effect of the residency decision is that states like California, with relatively high benefits, will bring pressure on Congress for some kind of national income maintenance program.

Our aim has been not only to increase dollar benefits, but to enable recipients to gain some control over the welfare system—to render it less arbitrary and oppressive. We have been able to reform procedures within the welfare department to bring them more in line with consititutional, due process requirements. One of the cases, in which we have challenged the failure of the state to give recipients a hearing before their benefits are cut off, is now before the United States Supreme Court. In a sense, however, everything we've done in the welfare area has been calculated to maintain constant pressure on the system to maximize its responsiveness to the poor. We have in part succeeded. We have shaken up the system and even encouraged many on the inside to make changes they felt they could not make before.

The retiring director of the state Department of Social

Welfare acknowledged the impact of our efforts, and those of other poverty lawyers in California, in the statement he gave at his final news conference on November 28, 1969:

Here in California we have been challenged on dozens of issues, all of them coming back to the fact that for the first time, the poor have real and effective advocacy in our courts. This, again, is the significant point transcending all other considerations and consequences. An era of advocacy has begun out of which, I am sure, public assistance is never going to be the same. Not only is this happening through the courts, but also in the meetings and hearings of welfare boards, advisory commissions and administrators at every government level. The poor have come out of their apathy, and our accountability for what we do and why we do it is theirs to know—as it always has been under the law but never before so vocally sought.

As I indicated earlier, one of the strategies for institutional change was promotion of economic development in the poverty community. The foundation was one of the first legal service programs to launch a serious undertaking in this area. The initial project, a laundromat in the Mission District financed with the first Small Business Administration loan in the West to a business owned and operated by poor persons, was highly successful. This venture led to the establishment of the San Francisco Local Development Corporation. (LDC) which was designed to serve as a catalyst in the development of other ghetto-owned enterprises, and eventually perhaps serve as a neighborhood development bank. This approach seemed to us to provide a more direct route to the redistributive goal than litigation. Although the LDC continues to function, and has assisted a number of ghetto residents in financing and managing new businesses, we have actually accomplished a great deal less over the past year or two in the economic area than we have in the courts. The slow pace of the LDC may be accounted for in part by staff problems and the time and energy that was consumed in obtaining initial funding. We also underestimated the difficulties in accumlating the capital and expertise necessary to move beyond the small retail or service business.

As we have seen, the foundation was initially conceived as a collection of largely autonomous neighborhood law firms with a central administrative staff to "keep the machinery running" and to provide liaison among the neighborhood offices and between them and the board and various outside agencies. This highly decentralized system was designed to insure maximum responsiveness to the particular needs of the various poverty communities.

I had become convinced from a brief study I had conducted for OEO in the summer of 1966 that a central research and planning staff was essential to implement the broader, strategic goals of the legal services program. Notwithstanding the greater dedication and competence of the attorneys in the OEO-funded agencies, I argued in my report that without structural changes that go beyond simply shifting the location of the office (into the neighborhood) there would be little difference in actual impact and operation between OEO legal programs and conventional legal aid. I suggested, therefore, a division of function between a central office and neighborhood offices. Lawyers in the central office would develop strategies for change and take the necessary steps to implement these strategies through test cases, class actions and the like. I contended that they should also maintain close relations with neighborhood organizations, "for the task of creative advocacy ought to reflect consultation with the slum community as well as feedback from the caseload of the neighborhood offices." The main task of the neighborhood office would be that "of serving a large volume clientele on something like a mass production basis," with some research and other assistance from the specialist attorneys.

Over the years, a strong central legal staff was built up in the Main Office of the foundation. The attorneys became specialists in housing and redevelopment, welfare and other areas, and they were responsible for the major cases of the foundation. The office was started with two attorneys. In the fall of 1969, there were approximately 15 attorneys (including most of the foundation's allotment of Reginald Heber Smith Fellows) and a total staff of about 25, not including the many law students working in the clinic program. The Main Office legal staff was now larger than any of the neighborhood offices. The Main Office attorneys were the "cosmopolitans" in the foundation: they were much more likely than the neighborhood attorneys to have contacts with other poverty lawyers across the United States—in OEO programs, the Legal Defense Fund—to attend regional and national conferences and training sessions and to keep up with the growing body of legal literature in their field.

From the very beginning, relations between the neighborhood offices and the Main Office were strained. In my report to OEO I had pointed out that one of the problems that might arise in setting up a separate structure for the strategic cases was

the tension between service to a mass clientele and creative advocacy. At any point the decision to allocate limited resources to a central planning staff may seem arbitrary, even heartless. For the decision will necessitate turning away desperate people who are, after all, entitled to the service. But unless this is done, little will be accomplished for the large majority of slum dwellers, and many of those who are served will receive only temporary relief.

Neighborhood attorneys felt that they were carrying the burden of providing legal services to the poverty community with little or no help from their Main Office colleagues. The latter were viewed as an expensive luxury —their case loads immorally small, the pace of their work annoyingly relaxed and the results highly dubious. Was the WACO case really worth all the time and effort that had gone into it, and what about the welfare cases that put a few more dollars in a recipient's pocket, if that? Is it fair to spend such a large share of the foundation's resources on these highly speculative cases when there are clear, tangible results obtained in eviction cases and divorce cases, where people really hurt? These questions bothered many neighborhood attorneys. Their growing resentment of Main Office attorneys was hardly diminished by the incidental benefits they seemed to enjoy—the many trips to conferences and meetings, the publicity in the newspapers and on television.

From the point of view of the Main Office attorneys, neighborhood lawyers were not only essentially engaged in a band-aid operation, but even on a remedial basis were frequently unable to give effective representation to their clients, given the unwillingness of the neighborhood offices either to limit caseloads or to accept more efficient, routinized procedures. Furthermore, several chief counsels were viewed as the prime perpetuators of a system in which the client community was often the loser.

Main Office attorneys were also unhappy about what appeared to be the political restrictions on some neighborhood offices. The principal example was the unwillingness of the Western Addition office to represent WACO in its fight with the Redevelopment Agency. This decision, it was felt, was motivated in part by a reluctance to oppose the black Establishment in the Western Addition (including the local EOC leaders) which supported redevelopment in exchange for more jobs for blacks in the agency and sponsorship of projects within the renewal area. Similarly, the Chinatown office was extremely reluctant to take an aggressive position against established interests in Chinatown. Thus it was fully two years before any action at all was taken against the sweatshops. It was no accident that these were the two offices in which the local Establishment had most to do with the selection of the chief counsel.

Tensions were heightened by racial and ethnic differences. The Main Office legal staff has been predominantly white (it is interesting that a black lawyer who joined the staff has had little sympathy for the goals and methods of the office) and largely Jewish. Criticism of the Main Office has undoubtedly been affected by the feeling that it was inappropriate for white lawyers to be deciding what is best for poor blacks.

Although the neighborhood lawyers continued to be critical of the increase in staff at the Main Office and its failure to operate primarily as a back-up resource for them, an uneasy truce emerged between the neighborhood offices and the Main Office. The chief counsels agreed to leave the Main Office alone if it would not interfere in internal operations of the neighborhood offices. The sovereignty of the neighborhood offices was not to be trifled with. This was not a very happy solution. Indeed, it became increasingly difficult to effect even a modest degree of coordination. At stake was raising the quality of service in the neighborhood offices—and at the very least, preventing a deterioration in quality. This meant being able to do something about recruitment of attorneys, training of new attorneys and increasing office efficiency. Development of a rational recruitment program to take advantage of the foundation's nationwide reputation to attract top legal talent, particularly minority lawyers, simply was not possible with each office refusing to yield on its absolute power to hire and fire staff. A staff training program never really existed—some chief counsels resented the interference, and one refused to permit his attorneys to attend training sessions. Development of standard legal forms and office procedures, sharing of information on cases, research memos and briefs to avoid duplication of effort and to insure the best thinking or approach to a case—all of these seemed unattainable despite repeated campaigns to bring them about. In response to a grant condition from OEO, the director of litigation (who is in effect the chief counsel for the Main Office legal staff) drew up a minimal plan to insure that information or more important or unusual cases would be made available to him and to the chief counsels in advance of filing, but leaving final control over the cases in the hands of the chief counsels. For a long period the chief counsels for one reason or another were unwilling to consider the plan on its merits.

We were caught in a bind. Our efforts to assist neighborhood offices in raising the quality of service to clients were generally opposed as undermining the autonomy of the neighborhood offices. As a result, the neighborhood job got tougher—with increasing resentment against the Main Office and a lowering of the quality of service to the clients in the neighborhoods. The offices continued operating essentially as independent law firms. Within the offices there was no real division of labor or specialization. Attorneys handled as best they could whatever cases and matters came their way on their interview days. Case loads were large and becoming more burdensome as the backlog of unfinished cases slowly but surely built up. Work with neighborhood groups was confined mostly to incorporation of essentially paper organizations. Moreover, the staff became less experienced, given the tendency to fill vacant slots with younger attorneys. And there was little effective supervision, since in most offices the chief counsel was playing primarily a political role in the community, having turned over the day-to-day administration of the office to his senior staff attorney or senior secretary. Consequently, in spite of the dedication and ability of most neighborhood attorneys, the quality of the work product in general declined.

The goal of community control had been institutionalized in the autonomous neighborhood offices, while the aim of institutional change was embodied in the Main Office legal staff. It was obvious that the growing antagonism between these two structures in large measure represented a conflict between the two goals. The lawyer-founders had been wrong in assuming that control by the client community was a necessary condition for, let alone compatible with, a program of institutional change. We were unfortunately burdened with some romantic notions of the poor.

The neighborhood leaders, particularly those identified with the poverty program, were following an old pattern fashioned by other ethnic groups as they fought their way up the power ladder. These leaders were, by and large, not out to change or seriously challenge the system; they simply wanted to be cut in. They were willing to have an understanding with the older, white Establishment: in exchange for greater control of public programs aimed at helping the poor., and more control over jobs and other rewards for their constituents, they would keep the peace. The WACO suit was, of course, embarrassing: it was not until the Redevelopment Agency by its arrogance alienated its black allies in the Western Addition that the neighborhood leaders were able to openly support WACO's position.

It may well be the case that, with respect to their conception of legal services, the neighborhood leaders at this point are much closer to the conservative Republicans than to the militant white lawyers.

It is always possible, of course, that the neighborhood leaders may become radicalized—and the violent repression of the Panthers may be doing just that. And it is also possible that the young black lawyers coming out of the Reginald Heber Smith program may press for a more radical approach to legal services. Neither group, so far, however, seems to be prepared to move much beyond the issue of community control. The two principal demands of the black Reginald Heber Smith Fellows in a recent confrontation with OEO officials were higher salaries and control of the program.

By the spring of 1969 I was convinced that there would have to be some basic change in the structure of the foundation: although much of our work, particulary in housing and welfare, was beginning to pay off, the tensions within the foundation were becoming critical. The changes that would have to be brought about would necessarily mean limiting, if not doing away with, the autonomy of the neighborhood offices. In my view, this could only be accomplished by a black coordinator dedicated to institutional change, that is, by a militant black lawyer. I tried unsuccessfully for several months to find such a person. Finally, in October, having held the office for three years, and with a sense that we had accomplished in some ways a great deal more than I had ever expected, I resigned as coordinator of the foundation. It was now up to the board to find my successor, and hopefully a solution to our dilemma.

In December of 1969 my successor was chosen. The new coordinator is a black lawyer who had been a staff attorney in one of the neighborhood offices, and more recently held a top administrative post in the EOC. He is an able attorney, with a strong sense of professionalism and a flair for administrative efficiency. Although not unsympathetic to the aims and approach of the Main Office legal staff, he clearly represents the interests and perspective of the neighborhood offices. The tensions within the foundation should be significantly reduced, the divisions healed. I assume that the commitment to institutional change will gradually become weaker and that the Main Office legal staff will be reduced in size and given a different direction—to serve primarily as back-up resource for the neighborhood offices.

In retrospect, this probably represents the only solution that was realistically open to the foundation. Reorganization in the image of the Main Office legal staff would have brought the foundation into more direct and intolerable confrontations with the Establishment and would have seriously jeopardized neighborhood support. Perhaps at this point the main objective should be the survival of the foundation as a major institution serving the ghetto under ghetto control.

If the militant white lawyers move on, this should not be interpreted simply as a reaction to a shift in leadership and possible direction of the foundation. Some have become disillusioned with the capacity of the legal system to respond; others may be following new fashions. In one way or another, however, the old coalition will very likely be dissolved. Looking back, I suppose we have each used the other—the black professionals and neighborhood leaders have gained an organization, and we had the chance to put our theories into practice. Still, it's sad the partnership couldn't last.

The San Francisco Mystique

FRED DAVIS

Crossing the Bay Bridge for the first time and seeing the city's skyline ascend into shimmering view, one's immediate response is—how breathtaking! how boldly urban! and, for ex-New Yorkers like the writer, how much *like lower Manhattan!* (Would, though, there stood the Lady where squats Alcatraz.) But the echo of Manhattan, like so much else about San Francisco, is deceptive. Viewing the same skyline from the Marin County side of the Golden Gate Bridge or *au fond* from the "canyons" of Montgomery Street, one soon realizes that despite a recent burst of high-rise building, the skyscrapers are not that many, that clustered or that tall. The mirage of Manhattan migrated to the nation's distant shore is attributable to the city's many steep hills upon which even small skyscrapers will, depending on the obliqueness of the angle of vision, seem tall and densely concentrated. To be deceived, though, is not necessarily to be disappointed. And it is precisely this quality of mild deception (duplicity? ambiguity?)—the deception itself, neither its discovery nor the truth it veils—which, more than anything, underlies the San Francisco mystique.

That this nebulous thing, a mystique, "really exists" and that the city's vast tourism industry, by now perhaps San Francisco's largest, trades almost shamelessly on it can hardly be disputed. Witness, for example, a recent Gallup poll which reported that San Francisco is the favorite city of Americans, leading in popularity by a goodly margin such more populous, more economically thriving and even more culturally endowed metropolitan centers as New York, Washington, Chicago and—to the *schadenfreude* of San Franciscans—Los Angeles. But even if there were no Gallup poll to lend a kind of awkward substance to something so intangible as a mystique, one need only observe the platform-hanging cable car riders on Hyde Street, the besotted conventioneers stumbling from one North Beach topless club to the next or even the hippie émigrés (alas, no longer wearing flowers in their hair) loitering in now boarded-over store entranceways on Haight Street, to intuit that there is something more ineffable at play between the city and its visitors than conventional tourist appeal. (Not that San Francisco is in the least lacking in bird's-eye views or historic sites or that its official publicists neglect, out of some uncharacteristic sense of civic reticence, to trumpet, exploit and commercialize them.) But to attempt to even vaguely apprehend this "something more" is to again be drawn into the realm of deception.

To deceive requires, as every showman from Eden's serpent through the great Barnum himself knew so well, some yearning on the part of the audience to be deceived. The problem of the city's mystique then becomes—what are the shared dreams and collective illusions of modern Americans that lend themselves to the particular concatenation of places, persons and scenes that is San Francisco? What is there about the career of these dreams, the future of these illusions, that until they founder in disenchantment are, as by the green light at the end of Daisy's dock, kindled for a time by the city's implied promise of fulfillment? That, like Gatsby's, dreams and illusions do founder in San Francisco, perhaps more so than elsewhere, is attested to by the city's unusually high rates of suicide, alcoholism, divorce and drug addiction, the first reputed to be the highest in the country. (A sociologist friend, occasionally given to ponderous puzzlement over the seemingly obvious, once asked why it was that nearly all suicides from the Golden Gate Bridge hurled themselves from that side of the roadway facing the Bay and not from the side facing the Pacific Ocean? The answer given him by an impatient wag: "Dope, because nearly all of the suicides come from the city and that's the side of the bridge they're on when they get ready to jump. Besides, if they ran to the other side they could get killed by the oncoming traffic.")

This yearning to be deceived, this shared illusion which San Francisco feeds—in short, its mystique—is made up, as would be the case with anything so complex as a city, of many strands. Two of them will be dealt with here, the first bearing mainly on urban man's relationship to his natural environment, the second on his relations with fellow urban dwellers.

As for the first, there is most obviously the vision of urban beauty that the city calls forth, especially if by urban beauty we conceive of some organic balance of the natural and the man-made, the intended and the fortuitous, the old and the new, the familiar and the strange. Few, for example, would argue with the by now clichéd contention that there is hardly a major city in the world which can rival San Francisco in the sheer splendor of its natural setting. Within sight of water from almost everywhere, ringed by the green-beige mountains of the Pacific coastal range, its

Bay traversed by the ribbons of several graceful bridges, flecked by white sails and traversed by the pregnant passage of ocean-going ships, the broad prospect is one of constant color change, exciting visual rhythms and a dramatic baring of the sinews of the city's work and movement. For some, this extravagant panoramic indulgence of the yearning to grasp the complex essence of the city in an instant is enough. But for those of more apollonian temper, there are also the visual pleasures of the small, intimate and contained. Turn a corner, crest a hill or simply gaze from a back window and the eye is gently led in small graduated stages, much as in the paintings of the early Flemish masters, from a rear garden, to an oddly shaped smokestack, to the voyeuristic promise of a distant balcony, to rest finally on a strip of harbor and the small moving figures of longshoremen unloading a boat. The panoramic urban spread *and* the framed view, the tall buildings *and* the mountains, the machine *and* the garden—it is the still seemingly comprehensible playing out of this root dialectic of Western man that evokes in many the sense of San Francisco being a city fashioned to human scale, a city somehow spared the worst excesses of a mindless technological order.

But is it? And if it is, how long can it last, barring some dramatic reversal of established trends? Needless to say, there is no shortage of viewers-with-alarm in the local press, the area's colleges and universities, the community at large and even in the civic establishment who point agonizingly to what has come to sound like a trite catalogue of environmental woes, if only through sheer repetition.

□ *Smog.* Cleansed by strong diurnal winds off the ocean, the Bay Area has in the past suffered considerably less from this scourge than have other large urban areas. Recent years, however, have seen an alarming decrease in the number of smog-free days. Now the yellow-gray cloud hangs sullenly over the Bay much of the time, and on calm days the telltale symptoms of eye, nose and throat irritation are much in evidence.

☐ *Pollution* of the Bay and ocean shore through chemical and biological waste, making these great natural resources much less attractive to fisherman, beachgoers and the small number of bathers hardy enough to brave the cold waters.

☐ *Land fill* of the Bay's shoreline for industrial and residential purposes. If continued at the same rate as in recent decades, land fill would by the year 2000, according to some estimates, transform San Francisco Bay into a polluted creek. Indeed, it probably was some such apocalyptic vision that led recently to the formation of a grass roots citizens' organization named Save Our Bay Committee (SOB—cry or curse, or both?) which has since waged a heroic fight against further land fill of the Bay.

☐ The continuing *loss of open green and shoreline space* for subdivisions and highway construction.

☐ *Massive traffic congestion* in downtown and other built-up areas which, while possibly lessened in some marginal way by a successful citizens' revolt a few years back against further freeway construction in San Francisco, grows perceptibly worse by the week. The absence of a modern public transportation system hardly helps matters, although some relief is promised with the completion of the Bay Area Rapid Transit subway system scheduled for 1972 or thereabouts. But even many of those who previously looked forward enthusiastically to this long-delayed, financially mismanaged and suburb-sabotaged subway system now despair over whether it can make more than a minor difference in the area's traffic problem.

☐ The *upsurge of high-rise office-building* in downtown San Francisco. According to Herb Caen, the columnist for the *San Francisco Chronicle* who more than anyone acts the part of troubador, chronicler and Jewish mother to the city's elusive mystique, this development will soon "manhattanize" the skyline to such a point that only upper-story moguls will enjoy the view while all others are relegated to the ant heaps below.

It may well be, then, that this strand of the San Francisco mystique—the still fleetingly confirmed vision of some humane balance between city man and his natural environment—is, like many another twentieth-century illusion, fated for extinction. In the paradoxical nature of the case, perhaps the last and only hope rests exactly with the prophets of ecological doom who, among other things, seem on the verge of fomenting a social movement of unprecedented scope in American history. (On the basis of a preliminary study, the sociologist John Lofland estimates that there are some 100 "environmental improvement" organizations in the Bay Area alone, the vast majority of them having been formed during the past five years.) For if some prophecies are self-fulfilling, others are self-negating by virtue of the very concern and fear they arouse.

The urban man-nature strand of the San Francisco mystique is, as I have suggested, sustained in large part by the city's truly unique geographical setting. Not unique, although probably more important for illuminating the psychic texture of the mystique, is the other strand I mean to speak of, that emanating from certain historic, at times fugitive, American visions of man's life-career in the city. The disclaimer of uniqueness in this connection is made despite much that is unusual and colorful about San Francisco's past: the gold rush with its violent influx of ravaging forty-niners, the earthquake and fire of 1906 and so forth. These much publicized memories notwithstanding, they are at best peripheral to the other collective vision that animates the city's mystique. The imagery for this vision derives less from America's colonial past or even the nineteenth-century westward movement of native settlers than from the great tide of European and Oriental immigration which during the period 1850-1920 irrevocably transformed the urban American experience for generations to come. For, like New York, Boston, Philadelphia and Chicago before it, by the year 1890 San Francisco was, and to some extent remains, an improbable assemblage of different peoples, tongues, customs and ambiences.

Merely to state this, however, can barely begin to convey the moods and meanings associated with the late nineteenth- and early twentieth-century immigrants' experience of the large American city. And, judging by much of our contemporary art, literature, drama, criticism and even politics, it was that experience which formed the prime collective memories and metaphors by which successive generations have sought, perhaps in vain, to grasp the "reality" of the city. This urban imagery, as Anselm Strauss points out in *Image of the American City,* is an amalgam of many elements. There is the "mosaic of little worlds" (ethnic and socioeconomic, occupational and avocational) of which the Chicago sociologist Louis Wirth wrote. There is, too, the experience of growing up in the city and moving between and among the boundaries of these little worlds so that parochial perspectives are shaken and new life possibilities spring to mind—an inner journey of adventure beautifully captured by Alfred Kazin in his poignant memoir *A Walker in the City.* Further, and contrary to a great deal of conventional criticism of the city as a place of heartless impersonality, there is the anchoring sense of neighborhood: of little stores and known people on familiar streets, of the memory of old gangs and the marvel over the diverse life routes charted by their members—in sum, that quality of primary feeling, especially in the ethnic enclaves of the city, whose apparent loss is bemoaned by such romantic critics of "functional" urban planning as Jane Jacobs. Most of all, perhaps, there is the mythic promise, writ large for the urban immigrant generations, of America itself—of personal change and discovery, of achievement, fame and upward mobility, of coming to approximate in a lifetime that strange and undefinable figure "the American" while somehow remaining, in line with Kenneth Burke's definition of piety, loyal to the sources of one's being.

These admittedly ambiguous and even partially contradictory themes form a master literary plot, as it were, with which recent generations of Americans (both the children of the immigrants and many nonimmigrant descendants as well) try to order in imagination the perhaps by now impossibly diffuse phenomenology of the American city. And it is because San Francisco lends itself so visibly to the symbolic imagery of this plot that its mystique is sustained, as much for émigrés from older eastern and midwestern cities as for its comparatively small number of native sons and daughters.

There still remains, after all, an authentic Chinatown where one can go on a Sunday for a family dinner and afterwards browse through the curio shops on Grant Avenue. (Secreted among the restaurants, shops and tenements there are also sweatshops where recent immigrants from Hong Kong toil at sewing machines for incredibly low piece rates. But, never mind, isn't this too part of the great immigrant experience in the American city?) There is a large Japanese settlement in the Western Addition, Russians and Poles along Clement Street, sizable Italian neighborhoods in North Beach and the Marina, a small French colony on outer Geary Boulevard, German, Irish and Mexicans in the Mission and blacks in the Fillmore and Hunters Point, although few whites now venture into these precincts. Oddly enough, there are no distinctive Jewish neighborhoods in San Francisco to speak of, this undoubtedly being due to the large East European Jewish immigration of the turn of the century never having quite reached San Francisco as it had, for example, New York, Boston, Chicago and, a generation later, Los Angeles.

Along with the ethnic neighborhoods per se there is the whole mélange of "non-American" locales and institutions to further accent the polyglot impress of the city. For example: the Chinese New Year's Parade which, in addition to the famous block-long cloth dragon, includes in its ranks an Armenian drum and bugle corps from as far away as Fresno; the old Italian men playing *bocce* on boxed-in strips of dirt court while chomping away on crooked black cigars; the many small foreign restaurants in which seven-course family style dinners are served at remarkably modest prices.

With all the ethnic variability, there is at the same time no dearth of characteristically American scenes, places and moods (many "redolent of an earlier era") to sustain the symbolic plot of a romantic, ultimately ennobled melding of the foreign and the native. It has been estimated, for example, that San Francisco contains more bars and taverns per square mile than does any other major American city. People other than tourists still ride the remaining cable cars to get to and from work every day. Ice cream can still be bought on sugar cones. Downtown there are still several old-fashioned, wood-paneled restaurants (a few with curtained-off private booths) in which gruff, white-aproned waiters hurl heaping plates at the patrons. (Unlike elsewhere, the displacement of waiters by waitresses has not progressed nearly so far in San Francisco.) Neither is the city unmindful of its Victorian past and the residue of charmingly functionless housing left over from that era; one is forever running across some many-gabled monster in the process of meticulous reconstruction by a band of talented homosexuals who plan, of course, to sell it eventually for an exorbitant sum. (Have urban planners needlessly overlooked a natural opportunity for encouraging self-generating urban redevelopment—to wit, subsidizing platoons of homosexuals and setting them loose in the more dilapidated areas of the city?)

But, as with the ecological threats that are rapidly demystifying the man-nature symbolism of the San Francisco mystique, so with the sociological threats that are gradually dispelling the immigrant-borne vision of a higher social harmony through heterogeneity. For there is little to indicate that San Francisco will escape the political, fiscal and racial plight that has already engulfed other large American cities. According to the most recent city population estimates prepared by Mildred Holota, chief of records and statistics for the San Francisco Health Department, one sees here as elsewhere:

☐ the same overall loss of central city population, from 740,000 in 1960 to 707,000 today, a loss for the decade of roughly 5 percent (San Diego has already displaced San Francisco as California's second most populous city);

☐ the same exodus of middle-and working-class whites to the suburbs, the in-city white population having declined from 604,000 to 504,000 during the past decade, a loss of better than 15 percent.

☐ the same inversely correlated increase in the central city black and other nonwhite minority populations; Negro population, for example, grew from 74,000 in 1960 to 102,000 today.

☐ the same distortion in the city's class structure, it becoming more and more a place for only the very rich and the welfare poor.

The dreary array of urban social problems to which these demographic trends point are by now too familiar to require even mention here. They are more than adequately discussed in, among other readily available documents, the Kerner Commission report. Suffice it to say that it is hard to imagine how any mystique, no matter how deep its cultural and historic roots, can long survive the crushing weight of such problems, especially since there is so little to suggest that the problems are being met or ameliorated to any significant extent.

At the same time, however, it is of the essence of mystiques that they persevere long after the symoblic plots they harbor fall afoul of the actions of the players and the credibility of the props. Thus, they retain a potential for shaping the future, much as they are given to mythologizing the past. It is on this perhaps deceptive and Delphian note then that one is in the end constrained to still accord a measure of "reality" to the San Francisco mystique.

NOTES ON CONTRIBUTORS

Michael Alexander   "San Francisco: A Photographic Portfolio"

A free-lance photographer in San Francisco. His work has appeared in *Time, Look, transaction* and other major magazines; he has had a one-man exhibition at the FOCUS gallery in San Francisco.

Howard S. Becker   "The Culture of Civility"

Professor of sociology at Northwestern University. He is well known for his studies of deviant behavior and social control. (For more detail, see the back cover.)

Jerome E. Carlin   "Store Front Lawyers in San Francisco"

A lawyer and a sociologist who besides teaching has served as consultant for legal projects and coordinator of the San Francisco Neighborhood Legal Assistance Foundation, 1966-1969. He has recently taken up the art of painting full time.

Fred Davis   "The San Francisco Mystique"

Professor of sociology at the University of California Medical Center in San Francisco. He is the author of *Passage through Crisis: Polio Victims and Their Families* (1963), and editor of *The Nursing Profession: Five Sociological Essays* (1966).

Ernest A. Dernburg   "The Health of Haight-Ashbury"

A psychiatrist in private practice in San Francisco and former psychiatric director of the Haight-Ashbury Free Medical Clinic. He has written and lectured widely in the fields of adolescent psychiatry, drugs and related matters.

Arthur E. Hippler
                    "The Game of Black and White at Hunters Point"

Associate professor of anthropology at the Institute of Social, Economic and Government Research at the University of Alaska. His current research interests are in the acculturation of Alaskan Eskimos and Indians and in transcultural psychiatric research. He is completing a book on the Hunters Point ghetto in San Francisco and editing two other books on Eskimo acculturation.

163

Irving Louis Horowitz   "The Culture of Civility"

Professor of sociology and chairman of the department at Livingston College, Rutgers University. He is editor-in-chief of *trans*action and director of *Studies in Comparative International Development*. Among his major books are *The Rise and Fall of Project Camelot, Professing Sociology* and *Three Worlds of Development*.

John Luce   "The Health of Haight-Ashbury"

Associate editor of San Francisco Magazine and public affairs director of the Haight-Ashbury Free Medical Clinic. He is also a student at the University of California Medical Center, in San Francisco.

Stanford M. Lyman   "Red Guard on Grant Avenue"

Associate professor of sociology and social psychology at the University of Nevada. With Marvin Scott, Lyman is the author of *Sociology of the Absurd* and *Agony and Ecstacy: Notes on Student Revolution*.

David E. Smith   "The Health of Haight-Ashbury"

Assistant clinical professor of toxicology at the San Francisco Medical Center and medical director of the Haight-Ashbury Free Medical Clinic. He co-authored, with John Luce and Ernest A. Dernburg, *Love Needs Care: A History of the Haight-Ashbury Free Medical Clinic, an Analysis of Its Patients and an Examination of Their Drug and Health Problems*.

Frederick M. Wirt   "The Politics of Hyperpluralism"

Research political scientist at the Institute of Governmental Studies and lecturer at the School of Education, University of California, Berkeley. He is the author of *Politics of Southern Equality: Law and Social Change in a Mississippi County* and he is currently preparing a study of the politics of San Francisco.